This book shows us that it truly is possible to be a successful business leader and an aware, compassionate human being. If you are wanting to find a way to authentic happiness and leadership effectiveness this is a great resource.

—Gordon Cairns, chairman, Woolworths Limited and Origin Energy

The Mindful Leader is a not-to-be-missed read. Michael Bunting breaks new ground, adding an important dimension to our understanding of leadership and the practice of leading. He offers insights about mindfulness that clearly illustrate how leadership development begins within, and he brings science to mindfulness in a way that offers practical applications for meeting today's leadership challenges—and for making an extraordinary difference in the world.

—Jim Kouzes and Barry Posner, co-authors of the award-winning book, *The Leadership Challenge*

We know self-aware leaders consistently achieve the best long term results for themselves and for others. This practical and insightful book is an excellent guide to developing extraordinary levels of self-awareness. Read it, apply its lessons and your leadership and life will be so much better for it.

—Shaun McCarthy, chairman, Human Synergistics, Australia & New Zealand

What I greatly appreciate about Michael Bunting's new book is that it reveals the value of honesty, truthfulness and integrity, not as a matter of right or wrong, but as an essential aspect of highly effective leadership. If all those in leadership positions around the globe took *The Mindful Leader* as a guide for their work, the results would be impressive.

—Sharon Salzberg, author of *Lovingkindness* and *Real Happiness at Work*

Our world needs a new kind of leader. The old paradigms of power, fear and control just don't work in our modern economy anymore. We need leaders who know how to inspire through vision, integrity, sustainability and compassion. If you are interested in finding out how to become a leader for the new economy this is a great read.

—Jostein Solheim, CEO, Ben & Jerry's

I have worked with Michael specifically in the area of Mindful Leadership and can say with confidence that Michael is the real deal. His deep understanding of the subject is second to none, and his methodology is disciplined and impactful. This book is an extraordinary resource for all leaders aiming to realise their true potential.

—Brian Gladsden, Country President and Managing Director, Novartis Australia and New Zealand

Michael Bunting is at the cutting edge of a new wave of business leadership that is developing more conscious, responsible, and dynamic organizations. His brilliant book shows us that outward success and a life of integrity and compassion are completely compatible, and that a deeper integration of our outer and inner lives is necessary for the future of our planet. This is a book for all those who truly wish to find a way to live and lead more consciously in the business world.

—Russ Hudson, co-author of *The Wisdom of the Enneagram* and collaborator for The Awakened Company

Leading in a way that leaves a positive legacy for generations to come should be the benchmark by which we measure great leadership. Conscious leadership is a requisite characteristic of any person who wishes to harness the potential of a millennial team. This book is a beautiful reminder of what that kind of leadership looks like and how to practice it.

—John Replogle, CEO, Seventh Generation

I have worked with Michael Bunting for several years. The message in this book reflects the way he lives and teaches—mindfully and insightfully. This book is a wonderful guide on exactly how to fully integrate mindfulness into your life and leadership. Science now tells us that mindfulness has a great impact on personal effectiveness, which in turn is not only good for you, but also for those you lead.

—**Jan Pacas, MD, Hilti Australia,**
2015 AHRI CEO of the Year

The Mindful Leader outlines the practices and disciplines that we see in the most effective and successful leaders. A really insightful and useful read for those wanting a practical guide for truly constructive leadership.

—**Andrew Reeves, CEO, George Weston**
Foods Australasia

The world, more than ever, needs mindful leaders. What are the leadership qualities and attributes that are fostered by mindfulness? How can they be brought about? This outstanding book by Michael Bunting, based on his deep understanding of leadership development as well as the science and practice of mindfulness, provides the answers to those and many other related questions. Read it or give it to people who need to read it.

—**Dr Craig Hassed, author of** *Mindfulness for Life*

I believe that being a great leader and a great human being are inseparable. This book beautifully shows us how to do both; to be not only the best leader in the world, but to be the best leader for the world. Reading *The Mindful Leader* and applying its lessons will enrich your life, your leadership, and the lives of all those you influence.

—**Rachel Argaman, CEO, TFE Hotels, Telstra National**
Corporate Businesswoman of the Year

Michael Bunting does a fantastic job of helping us not only learn how to practice mindfulness, but how to practice it in the pressurised and rapidly changing context of business leadership. If you apply the practices in this book it will not only make you a better person, it will transform your leadership and your business.

—Angus Kennard, Kennards Hire Group

As business is waking up to the sustainability revolution, so too must leaders embrace a new, deeply mindful kind of leadership. This book will guide you on how to be the kind of leader that this planet needs now more than ever. The kind of leader and human being your children would be proud of.

—Ryan Honeyman, author of *The B Corp Handbook*

Free Bonus Resources

To get the most out of this book, make sure you download your free resources and companion workbook at www.mindfulleaderbook. com/bonus

THE Mindful LEADER

THE Mindful LEADER

7 Practices for Transforming
Your Leadership, Your Organisation
and Your Life

MICHAEL BUNTING

WILEY

First published in 2016 by John Wiley & Sons Australia, Ltd

42 McDougall St, Milton Qld 4064
Office also in Melbourne

Typeset in 12/14 pt Bembo Std, by Aptara, India

© Worksmart Australia Pty Ltd atf Worksmart Australia t/a WorkSmart Australia 2016

The moral rights of the author have been asserted

National Library of Australia Cataloguing-in-Publication data:

Creator:	Bunting, Michael, author.
Title:	The Mindful Leader: 7 practices for transforming your leadership, your organisation and your life / Michael Bunting.
ISBN:	9780730329763 (pbk.)
	9780730329770 (ebook)
Notes:	Includes index.
Subjects:	Leadership.
	Executive coaching.
	Success in business.
	Mindfulness (Psychology)
Dewey Number:	658.4092

Cover Design by Wiley/Kristin Bryant
Cover Images by Water Ripple: © ProMotion/Adobestock;
Graphs: © sebra/Adobestock; Paper Boat: © endrews21/Adobestock;
Leaves: © silverspiralarts/Adobestock
Composite Image by Kristin Bryant

Printed in USA by Quad/Graphics

10 9 8 7 6 5 4 3 2 1

Disclaimer

To my three children.

My deepest hope is that this book will make the world a better place, so your generation's future is filled with consciousness, kindness, connection and sustainability.

Contents

About the author

Michael Bunting is the founder of the leadership consultancy WorkSmart Australia, a certified B Corp. He has trained and coached thousands of leaders, from CEOs to front-line leaders. WorkSmart consults to organisations ranging from global multinationals through to medium-sized businesses in the area of leadership, engagement, alignment, values and culture. He is the author of *A Practical Guide to Mindful Meditation* and co-authored *Extraordinary Leadership in Australia & New Zealand* with Jim Kouzes and Barry Posner, the world's premier researchers and authors in the field of leadership. He also teaches Mindful Leadership for Sydney University's award-winning Global Executive MBA.

Michael regularly contributes articles for industry magazines including *CEO Magazine*, *BRW*, *SmartCompany* and *Inside HR*. He has also appeared on Sky Business News and several radio stations. He delivers large-scale keynote presentations at industry events, trade shows and company off-sites.

Michael has run a disciplined personal mindfulness practice for more than 23 years and has taught mindful leadership to businesses and government for more than 16 years. Michael holds two business degrees and a postgraduate diploma in mindfulness-based psychotherapy.

He lives with his family in Sydney, Australia.

Introduction

How mindfulness impacts leadership

One can have no smaller or greater mastery than mastery of oneself.
Leonardo da Vinci

When I started my personal transformation journey at the age of 22, fresh out of studying business at university, I had no idea what I was signing up for. I was starting what seemed like a cool process of gathering knowledge by taking evening classes in practical philosophy, depth psychology and mindfulness meditation. I thought this would somehow make me special.

What I did not realise at the time was how delightfully humbling the process would be—that it would bring me into direct, truthful contact with my confusion, my deep conditioning, my self-obsession, my painful insecurity, my need to feel validated by always being 'right'... and so much more. Rather than making me special it exposed a wonderful ordinariness in me.

Now, as I look back on years of disciplined mindfulness practice, the inquiry processes, the failures and successes, the laughter and the tears, I see that mastery of oneself is more about removal than addition. It's about stripping off the masks and pretences that keep us feeling isolated. It's about letting go of beliefs and ideas that keep us locked in self-defeating habits. It's about dissolving the inner judge, surrendering the burden of a busy mind, and rediscovering the innate love and wisdom that have been with us all along. It's a mastery that clears the conditioned patterns that confine us.

And as we let go, we begin to connect with our deepest, truest selves. In a sense, we take Pinocchio's journey. We become real and authentic, and our artificial selves fade away. As the parts of us that we want to hide from ourselves and the world are revealed, we are empowered to fully embrace our whole selves. This is how we find authentic joy and meaning in our lives.

What is mindfulness?

I define mindfulness as *maintaining an open hearted awareness of our thoughts, emotions, bodily sensations and environment in the present moment.* It is paying attention in the present moment purposefully, warm-heartedly and non-judgementally. It is experiencing and accepting the present moment as it really is — not how we want it to be, think it should be or perceive it to be, but as it really is.

Kevin Pickhardt, the CEO of Pharos, a print management solutions company headquartered in New York, gave me his beautiful definition of mindfulness: 'Being mindful is our ability to pay attention and respond to every situation in the healthiest way possible — to accept whatever happens and respond with kindness, compassion and understanding.'

Through meditation and other practices we become more aware of our habitual reactions, expand the gap between stimulus and response and make wiser choices. We learn to see the innermost motivations for our actions and become more honest with ourselves. We learn to be the observer of our thoughts, rather than identifying with them and getting caught up in the mental stories we create. In short, we become profoundly self-aware.

The extensive research I will share with you in this book shows that mindfulness is not a new age, intangible abstraction for lofty-minded seekers of spiritual enlightenment. It is a concrete discipline proven to provide real, *measurable* benefits for your behaviour, performance, health and happiness. It is a well-developed, thoroughly substantiated, evidence-based process for gaining clarity and accessing and developing your greatest potential. As my friend and colleague Charlotte Thaarup-Owen, founder of the Mindfulness Clinic, puts it, 'Mindfulness practice enables us to gradually learn to use the mind just as a tool, rather than as a tool and an obstacle. Our past conditioning embedded in our mind often gets in our way and causes us to make poor decisions. Mindfulness trains the mind to become present so that we can greet every experience with wisdom and freshness and start responding instead of reacting.'

The integration of mindfulness and leadership

Within a few years of starting my journey with mindfulness I was fortunate to meet two wonderful mentors who taught me the connections between mindfulness and leadership. As mindfulness became my deepest passion, they invited me to teach and make a living from the work. This was at a time when very few organisations offered transformational leadership development programs, let alone mindfulness training. Back in the late nineties mindfulness was a radical idea, even stigmatised. I took a great risk when I left my own thriving paper merchant business and joined them in the trailblazing venture of teaching mindfulness and leadership to business and government.

But it worked, and far exceeded my expectations. The programs were radically successful. Before any research on mindfulness was available, people connected with the elegant common sense of mindfulness in a leadership and transformational context, and the results were usually life changing.

The key is the integration of mindfulness and leadership. Just being mindful is not enough. Even with serious mindfulness training we can still be poor leaders. But when mindfulness is fully integrated into leadership, exponential progress can be made. This book marries research-based mindfulness practices and leadership behaviours to provide a practical model for improving your leadership and your life. For me, that has been the greatest reward of this work — supporting leaders to *truly* transform themselves and their teams.

I don't think the leaders I've worked with had much idea what they were taking on when they said yes to authentic, mindful leadership and personal development. They did not realise that the familiar ground they were standing on would be shaken. We like the word *transformation*, but the process is a whole lot grittier than the advertising. As one of my favourite awareness teachers once put it, 'Most of us are not prepared to sign up for transformation, we just want to become a caterpillar with wings. But that is not a butterfly.' The caterpillar does not survive the process of becoming a butterfly.

Transformation is the territory of true leadership. The process of reinvention calls for a spirit of adventure. A transformational leader is willing to stay young, a beginner, an adventurer inside and out. They are also ordinary people. The work of true transformation is just that: work. It takes no special talent or skill. But it does take an uncommon determination to face our fears, reactivity, avoidance patterns and insecurities and to keep going. It takes strength.

Developing as a leader is about cultivating our inner strength to stay true under fire, to ask questions we don't know the answer to, to stay balanced when our world is turning upside down, to stay kind and respectful when the heat of anger and frustration is coursing through our veins, to courageously hold ourselves and others accountable when we want to slip into avoidance and self-justification. It is about enabling ourselves to connect with others with authentic compassion, to truly understand them, to see their struggles and aspirations, the deepest desires of their hearts, their greatest potential. And, perhaps above all, it is to stay real, to keep coming back to honesty and humility.

My friend Barry Keesan, Senior Vice President for General Code, a municipal codification service company in the US, explained to me how feedback is critical to this process. People are reluctant to give leaders feedback because they fear the consequences. This can create a skewed view of reality in the leader — it's easy to start believing you are perfect and everyone is engaged. That's a dangerous way to lead, especially if you are the last to know when your people are not truly aligned. So you have to really work at getting honest feedback.

Barry said, 'You have to make yourself vulnerable, admit your fears, mistakes and uncertainties, and communicate to people that you welcome honest feedback. And that sends a message that you value them, that their opinion matters and that you are humble enough to look at your own actions. For me, it's actually a validation that I am doing something right when my team gives me honest feedback. It's paradoxical, but true. It means I have a good relationship with my team when they tell me when I did something that was out of line.'

When I expressed my surprise at Barry's attitude, given how rare it is, he explained that what has enabled him to stay open is years of mindfulness practice. Mindful, inspiring leaders like Barry are authentic and courageous enough to put down their mask. They have found a deeper place of self-acceptance in themselves, an acceptance of their humanity. They know all too well their faults and failures. They rarely excuse them or rationalise them. When they go off track (as they inevitably will) they are willing to really listen to the feedback they receive. They are people we can trust and relate to. We warm to them because they have cultivated an awareness we are drawn to.

But don't misinterpret their kindness and authenticity for complacency or softness. They can be tough when they need to be. Their compassion can be fierce. They will hold you accountable for commitments and will not avoid the tough conversations. They will stretch you beyond your capacity.

Jeff Weiner, the CEO of LinkedIn, a strong advocate of mindful leadership and judged by one rating service to be the best CEO in the US, is a great example of this. When asked in an interview how he handles poor performance he replied, 'You do it in the most compassionate and most constructive way you know how.' Jeff then goes all in with those people to help them close their performance gap, and if it does not work out they are invited to leave, but with the support to find something better. As he put, 'And if it doesn't work out, we're gonna figure out another role for you here hopefully, and if that doesn't make sense, I'll do everything I can to make sure you're successful elsewhere.'[1]

The greatest leaders cultivate a paradoxical and profoundly effective combination of strength and compassion. It is less science than art. But make no mistake, the science backing mindfulness and its impact on leadership is incontrovertible.

Why does mindfulness matter for leadership and the bottom line?

A critical factor in creating and sustaining job satisfaction, productivity and a healthy bottom line is workplace engagement. Research firm Towers Watson reports that organisations with high rates of engagement consistently outperform their sector benchmarks for growth across a range of financials, including more than double the stock performance of the Dow Jones and Standard & Poor's Index for five years running. Great Place to Work's data shows that between 1997 and 2013 the best companies performed nearly two times better than the general market. Furthermore, the value of their 100 best companies grew by 291 per cent between 1998 and 2012. Compare that with the 72 per cent growth of the Russell 3000 Index and the 63 per cent growth of the S&P 500 Index. Great workplaces perform better and have substantially stronger bottom lines.

Leadership is the cornerstone of engagement. According to research performed by leadership experts Jim Kouzes and Barry Posner, my friends and co-authors of *Extraordinary Leadership in Australia and New Zealand*, nothing impacts engagement more than the behaviour of leaders. As much as 37 per cent of employee engagement can be attributed to the boss's leadership behaviour. Leading from and embodying values and integrity, inspiring a shared vision and common purpose, staying open to continually learning, challenging oneself and others, enabling and developing others, building trusting relationships and recognising others for great work—these exemplary leadership qualities produce tangible results.

Jim and Barry have analysed responses from more than 2.5 million people across the world and found that leaders who exhibit these behaviours have employees who are significantly more committed, proud, motivated, loyal and productive. In groups with exemplary leaders, engagement scores are 25 to 50 per cent higher than in other groups.[2] In one study, researcher and author Richard Roi looked at 94 large companies (with an average annual income of US$17.4 billion) and compared those in which senior leaders applied exemplary leadership behaviours to a greater extent with those companies applying them to a lesser extent. The companies with great leadership enjoyed an average stock price growth of 204 per cent over ten years and a net income growth of 841 per cent. For companies in which leadership behaviour was weak, the average stock price growth was 76 per cent, and their net income decreased by 49 per cent.

Note that these are behaviours, not technical competencies. When leaders fail, it is rarely related to technical competence. The x-factor in leadership is behaviour. And the key to transforming leadership behaviour is the cultivation of genuine mindfulness married with leadership research and practice. This enables you to truly see and manage your behaviour in real time, which is when it really matters.

Daphne Guericke, Vice President of Content Analytics at Appen Inc., a language technology consulting firm in Seattle, Washington, shared with me how mindfulness impacts her leadership behaviour on a daily basis. First and foremost, she said, it helps her to understand herself. It reveals her triggers and where her values may be misaligned. It helps her observe how she reacts to thing. As she put it, 'I need to be very aware and attentive to what's going on with *me* so I can be attentive, aware and present for others. We all have crazy lives and it's easy to just go, go, go, constantly fighting fires and dealing with issues. Mindfulness practice ensures I don't lose myself or my values in the chaos. When I'm more present with people it creates a much more genuine interaction rather than just intellectual problem solving. It really helps me to connect with people on a deeper, more human level. We're all hungry for that because it's so easy to feel like a cog in a wheel in the corporate world.'

A number of research studies have proven how mindfulness has a measurable impact on behaviour. Cognitive neuroscience studies show that it actually creates structural and functional changes in the brain. Observed behaviour changes include:

- improved attention control

- improved self-awareness

- improved emotional regulation.

One study concluded, 'When engaged in cognitively demanding challenges, meditation is an effective means to "de-automate" behavior. We are less likely to respond with an impulsive/habitual response.'[3] Another judged, 'Mindful meditation will make you less mentally rigid and habit prone therefore more open to change.'[4] In yet another study, the researchers found, 'In a dynamic workplace setting, mindfulness may be a better predictor of workplace performance and job turnover than traditional measures of "engagement".'[5]

The equation is simple: Highly engaged organisations are more profitable and effective. The key to improving your organisation's engagement is your leadership behaviour. And mindfulness — the practical application of self-awareness — is the most effective method for recognising and improving your behaviour.

In this book you will discover simple and advanced approaches to mindfulness practice and how to apply it skilfully and consistently, *specifically* in a leadership context. But like anything truly worthwhile, mindfulness is not a quick fix. The research shows that even small amounts of practice help, but to reach your full potential will take more than a few minutes. It will take a deep understanding of the nuances of mindfulness practice and exactly how it applies to leadership. It is a profoundly rewarding journey though—it will challenge you to your core, in the very best way. It can set you free from the behavioural patterns that are getting in your way, some of which you may not even be aware of yet.

This book will equip you with a proven methodology for holding yourself accountable. It teaches you how to skilfully become real and honest with yourself in a way that holds nothing back. It gives you a clear understanding of how to expose your blind spots and overcome your fears and self-defeating habits.

But more importantly, throughout the process you'll learn how to treat yourself with kindness and compassion so that your new understanding is liberating and joyful, rather than simply painful. And when you learn to manage yourself with strength and kindness, you'll be empowered to use the same qualities when leading others. You'll be able to firmly hold people accountable for values and commitments in a way that builds and develops them, rather than tearing them down. You'll cultivate the skill you need to handle difficult situations with a paradoxical—and incredibly effective—combination of total honesty and genuine care. In short, you will realise your full potential as a leader.

If you want a quick fix, a simple technique to make discomfort disappear and the leadership journey easy, you will find little of value in this book. If, however, you are interested in what da Vinci refers to as the greatest mastery of all, then this book will help you achieve your full potential.

I invite you to enter this journey home to yourself, to your deepest longing for aliveness, authenticity, happiness, meaning—and leadership greatness.

Chapter 1

Be here now

The faculty of voluntarily bringing back a wandering attention over and over again, is the very root of judgment, character, and will. No one is [competent] if he have it not. An education which should improve this faculty would be the education par excellence.

William James, *The Principles of Psychology*, 1890

I once heard the great Vietnamese Zen teacher Thich Nhat Hanh say, 'When we are well, our wellness spills onto others. And when we are unwell, that too spills onto others. Be well.' The behaviour of leaders has an enormous impact on those they lead, and the more senior they are the greater the impact. Leadership is both a privilege and a burden. It is incumbent on leaders to be well and to lead from a centre of wellness and non-reactivity. Leaders set the tone for the whole team or organisation: when they are calm, confident, open and relaxed, the team is more likely to feel the same. Likewise, when they are stressed, fearful and closed, it breeds the same emotions among team members.

In later chapters we will cover the integrated mindful practices that support specific leadership development challenges. But before we get into the subtleties of this transformational practice, we'll start with some basics so we can build from the ground up.

I usually start mindfulness foundation training by asking leaders an open-ended question: 'What state are you in when you are at your best as a leader?' The answers are remarkably consistent: Physically, they are relaxed, rather than tense. Mentally, they are clear and calm, as opposed to being plagued by racing, frantic thoughts of regret, doubt and worry. Emotionally, they feel openhearted and courageous, as opposed to closed, hardened or fearful. Of course, this state is vital not only for great leadership but in all areas of our lives. Interestingly, most leaders agree that this state is in fact what we yearn for the most. It's the promise behind all our goals and longings.

So *how* can we deliberately cultivate healthy physical, emotional and mental states and become the captain of our own ship in this respect? How can we manage our internal world regardless of what is happening in our external world? Being dependent on external conditions for our inner wellbeing creates a constant underlying angst because we have little, if any, control over our external world. We can influence it, but we can't control it.

> *Mindful leadership means deliberately cultivating a state of wellness and being a beacon of goodness, responsiveness and clarity, even in the toughest circumstances.*

Absentmindedness: the opposite of mindfulness

The first step toward managing anything is to be aware of what it is we're trying to manage. Try tidying up a room in the dark: it's obvious we cannot manage what we cannot see clearly and objectively. In the case of mindful leadership, we're trying to manage our state: our body, mind and heart, and by extension our words, actions, behaviours and habits. Using the previous analogy, what keeps the room 'dark' is absentmindedness.

Most of us spend a substantial amount of time lost in thoughts about the future and the past. The science is clear that this habit is damaging for our health and wellbeing—particularly ongoing negative thinking ('I should have said ... ', 'Why did I forget that?', 'I hope my investments are going to be okay'). As one study concluded, '[A] human mind is a wandering mind, and a wandering mind is an unhappy mind. The ability to think about what is not happening is a cognitive achievement that comes at an emotional cost.'[1]

Absentmindedness, defined as being inattentive or distracted or zoning out, undermines our awareness and keeps us 'in the dark'. Put simply, we cannot be self-aware or truly aware of others when we are distracted by our thinking (mentally preparing our answer while someone is speaking to us, for example, or rehashing meetings or interactions in our mind). Over the years of teaching mindfulness to thousands of leaders I have invited them to put what they have learned to the test in their own context. Invariably they have found that awareness and absentmindedness are mutually exclusive, but their greatest shock is realising how much of their lives is spent in an absentminded state.

During an interview, neuropsychologist and bestselling author Dr Rick Hanson told me that being consistently lost in thought is one of the most damaging things we can do for our mental and emotional wellbeing and our brain health. Most of our thinking typically defaults to negative patterns—in part based on our collective biological history.

As Rick explained, the brain's negativity bias evolved because our ancestors lived when lethal dangers were real and ever present. In a world where the 'carrots' were sex, shelter and food and the 'sticks' were snakes, lions and injuries (which generally meant death), it paid to focus on the sticks. If you missed a carrot today, you'd have another chance tomorrow. But if you missed a stick, well, no more carrots ... ever.

In the modern world life-threatening situations are relatively unusual. But given our natural tendency to focus on the negative, combined with a habit of inattention and being lost in thought, we spend much of our time in a mentally constructed fight, flight or freeze mode. This unnecessary and inappropriate activation response leads to our accumulating wear and tear of the body and mind—called allostatic load—which is a major cause of physical and mental health problems, including depression, anxiety and stress-related illnesses. In the context of leadership, the negativity bias and allostatic load rob us of self-awareness and energy, over-focus us on threats and make it harder to learn from positive experiences. It's like wanting our brain to perform like a Ferrari while we drive it through the mud every day.

We are all well-practised experts in absentmindedness. We can eat, drink, sit through meetings pretending to listen—all while fixated on our own thoughts about the past and future. We can arrive at our destination in the car and not recall the journey at all. The critical point is that absentmindedness pulls us from reality, which prevents us from seeing things clearly, within ourselves or others. It's a thoroughly ingrained habit for most of us.

A deeper way to look at this subject is to examine the three underlying ways we lose connection with reality:

1. **Resistance/Avoidance:** This is an 'anything but this experience' attitude. It can manifest as fear, anxiety, worry, procrastination, avoidance, frustration, irritation, complaining, arguing, judging, even hostility or hatred. Things are not good enough or safe enough for us. Our thoughts can be mildly resistant ('I wish it wasn't so dull today!') to intensely resistant ('I can't stand anyone who disagrees with me!'). There is a definite sense of argument, and mild to extreme unease with our life as it is (or was). That argument with our life adds unnecessary stress to our system.

2. **Clinging/Idealisation:** Children know this one very well: 'Are we there yet?' As adults we play the 'I'll be happy when...' or the 'When...then...' game. We are unconsciously restless and dissatisfied with what is in front of us. But instead of focusing on the negative, we yearn for the 'next ideal thing'—that next promotion, car or holiday house. 'When I get x, then I'll be happy!' This sets up an endless quest for the ideal experience—we want the room neither too hot nor too cold, and if it's not just right (which

it very rarely is) we suffer and crave a more ideal experience. Another aspect of clinging is greed. We cling to prized possessions, people, ideas, prejudices, jobs, status. In that clinging there is a fear of loss, and therefore a consistent stress in our system.

3. **Delusion/Numbing:** We can call this zoning out or becoming numb. It does not have the aliveness or strong 'itch' of the other two, but it is very much a form of absentmindedness. It's a deadening of ourselves. This could be as simple as overeating, drinking too much alcohol, excessive TV watching or overusing our phones, for example. But on a more subtle level it is a kind of habituation, a sense of neutral passivity. Things aren't fresh or alive or exciting, they are just kind of okay. Daydreaming is a good example of zoning out, as is driving your car to work on autopilot and not remembering the journey.

Sadly, I have worked with too many good people who have become numb, burned out or alienated from their families and their team members as a result of a steady diet of clinging, avoidance and numbing. In their quest for success they have indulged in endless worry, obsessive planning, values compromises, aggression and more. Eventually they come to recognise that these habits cannot produce the inner wellbeing they long for, and their lives are living evidence of this.

Ironically, the deep and personal longing behind their business goals—happiness, a clear mind, an open connected heart, a sense of wellbeing—progressively decreases as their bank balance increases. This relentless sense of dissatisfaction and stress is not success. Yet it is possible to gain both outer success and inner wellbeing.

Presence: the antidote

We can overcome the detrimental effects of absentmindedness by learning to cultivate our capacity to be truly present to what is happening in ourselves and the world in real time.

Through mindfulness we develop, both internally and externally, a clear-eyed view of the world. We see reality as it is, not as we want or don't want it to be. We are present to what is happening in front of us, right now, at this very moment: the breath under our nose, the colours in the room, the texture of our clothes. Right now is real. Everything else is memory of the past or imaginings of the future. Reality is always *now*. And mindfulness is living and being fully present in the now.

Descriptions of people who convey how they feel when they are truly focused in the present, and who have relinquished all thoughts of the past or future, are strikingly familiar: calm, clear, open-minded, open-hearted, relaxed, engaged, productive, 'in flow'. As one of my clients, Kim Phillips from the pharmaceutical company AbbVie, put it, 'It is such a relief when I remind myself that I can only be here now. When the workload is overwhelming I remember that the best thing I can do is just be present and do what is in front of me. It is so incredibly helpful. The stress melts away and I become so much more productive.'

It's the answer to the question with which I start all my foundation mindfulness training courses: *What state are you in when you are at your best as a leader?* I have been privileged to witness this 'a-ha' moment in thousands of people in my programs, and it's really quite simple: *Being present and being at your best are one and the same thing.*

Presence is both the end we're all seeking and the means of achieving it. When we're present, we're able to manage ourselves. It's only when we're present that we truly have the gift of choice — otherwise we're ruled by habit. The irony is that, more often than not, in our desperate search for the benefits of presence, we do everything but stay present.

Being mindful of the present moment allows us to observe and experience painful emotions without being sucked into them or allowing our behaviours to be dictated by them. It releases us from the oppression of incessant thoughts. It sheds light on things we've been resisting and gives us the courage to stop resisting. When we learn to see and experience what is happening clearly in the present moment we notice things that make us think to ourselves, 'How did

I ever miss that?' or 'Why have I been acting like that for so long?' More than that, we also see the goodness and beauty in ourselves that we've buried under layers of self-criticism and shame. The beauty of real presence is that it reveals ourselves to ourselves — not through theory, but in reality. It is a self-transforming practice.

Sometimes the insights that come from mindfulness are painful. But as Socrates said, 'The unexamined life is not worth living.' Or as psychologist Dr Phil McGraw put it, 'Better to be awakened by a painful truth than lulled to sleep by a seductive lie.' The brief pain we may feel from a mindful realisation is far more desirable than the endless struggle we experience from remaining unmindful.

The objective and underlying purpose behind mindfulness is to rid ourselves of all mental and emotional stress. It's not about being present for the sake of it, but rather about ending the suffering that ensues from not being present. In other words, mindfulness is a means, not an end. And that is not just to end our own suffering, but to alleviate the suffering of others as well. By choosing to act in a spirit of mindfulness we simultaneously help ourselves while contributing to a more peaceful, healthy and whole planet for everyone. It brings much deeper meaning to business leadership than simply growing the bottom line. It's not melodramatic to say that your work as a leader can have a profound impact on the evolution of humanity.

Mindfulness is much more than observation

It's often said that mindfulness means observing our current state non-judgementally. That's certainly part of it, yet it can imply that we're not actively involved in the process — that we're aloof from the experience. But in mindfulness we're both observing and involved. We are simultaneously observing and feeling our body, our emotions, our experiences. We are aware, paying deep, intimate attention to everything. Accepting the reality of the present is not resignation. It is a full embracing of what is.

When we are mindful, we observe what is happening in ourselves and around us without being possessed by it. But there is a counterpoint to observation. I practised being the 'observer' for my first ten years of mindfulness practice and slowly became disassociated and almost uncaring. I remember watching cruelty on the news and not being affected at all, feeling rather proud of how 'balanced' my response was. It was only later that I understood this was not mindfulness but rather dissociation, a fake form of inner balance. True mindfulness is paradoxical because it increases our sensitivity while at the same time increasing our inner balance and strength. So we are objective observers, but equally we are fully present and feeling what is happening.

Sue Kochan, the CEO of Brand Cool, an advertising firm based on the east coast of the US, spoke with me about how this feels in her. 'I don't get angry during stressful times,' she said, 'but I definitely feel fear. The only thing that has kept me from falling apart has been being able to go inside and to actually just look at the fear, to let it run its course. I let it do what it does, I feel it in my body, I watch it with my mind to see how it dances and changes. And when I allow myself to feel it, rather than simply transcend it through mere observation, I notice that it isn't so solid. If I make a lot of room for it and welcome it in, it actually dissipates. It loses its strength to hold me.'

Mindfulness isn't about moving away from or rising above our fears, insecurities and worries. Rather, it equips us with the strength to move toward them, embrace them and feel them fully—but without allowing them to dominate our lives. It is only by moving toward our sources of stress that we can really deal with them. Mindfulness is the means of doing so.

The purpose of mindfulness isn't to make us more stoic or dispassionate in the face of adversity and suffering. Rather, it is to make us more open, sensitive, tender, compassionate and caring. Perhaps a more accurate term for the purest form of mindfulness is *heartfulness*. The process connects us more authentically to the deepest yearnings of our heart. At the core of all our contracted defence mechanisms, such as anger, pride, avoidance and aggression, is a deep longing to be loved and to love.

In short, true mindfulness doesn't make us harder and more impervious; rather, it makes us softer and more vulnerable. And paradoxically, by so doing it actually makes us stronger. Our ego wants us to believe that there is strength in being invulnerable, when the truth is the opposite. Invulnerability is nothing but a false shield to protect us from difficult emotions. It keeps us isolated and disconnected. It is only by recognising, accepting and embracing our emotions that we become truly strong. With nothing left to fear and protect, we become free.

The senses: how to be present

The first and simplest step to developing genuine presence is to tune in to the first foundation of mindfulness: the senses.

It sounds simplistic, I know. Perhaps even a bit cheesy. But walk through a quick exercise with me to experience for yourself how many new things you can notice when you become present through the senses.

Breathe slowly through your nose. Focus on nothing but your breath. Notice that the temperature of the air is warmer when it comes out your nose than when it entered; the body warms the air up. Have you ever noticed this? Most people haven't, yet it has literally been right under their nose their whole life. Now tune in to your feet. Feel the pressure of your shoes on the floor. I'm betting this is the first time you've actually consciously tuned in to your feet today.

This simple exercise shows how tuning in to our senses makes us aware of things we've never noticed before. It's not really about breath or feet; it's simple proof that, through connecting with our senses, we can truly begin to see into every aspect of our experience: our body, mind, emotions, behaviours, habits and relationships. And once we can perceive our habits and thoughts objectively we are no longer ruled by them; we no longer blindly follow or believe them. This new insight enables us to manage them and our behaviour.

Tuning in to the senses is a powerful way to develop presence because the senses are experienced only in the present. You cannot smell two seconds from now or listen to a sound from ten seconds ago (the lingering memory of the sound is not the sound itself). The senses are immediate, alive, here now. It is impossible to be anywhere other than in the present when we are fully and completely connected with the senses. And we can usually be present only with one sense at a time—we may hear, then feel, then see, all in a sort of seamless dance in the present.

Michael von der Geest, a senior executive and consultant with the professional services firm Ernst and Young in the UK, explained to me how tuning in to his senses has helped him develop emotional intelligence in his work. When he focuses on his senses he feels like things slow down, which gives him greater clarity. Michael feels this is particularly important for him because he is conceptual and intuitive, and his mind moves fast, which can harm his relationships by preventing him from listening closely. When people start talking to him he's already thinking ahead to his reply. By tuning in to his breathing and grounding himself, he's able to sit and really listen.

More than just teaching him to listen, the process has taught him empathy, a critical leadership skill, as Michael explained: 'You can't do anything long term through a position of authority. You can only get people on board when you empathise with them and take them on a journey with you. You have to get people together and get a consensus, and my job is to influence that outcome. I can't just shove my vision down from the top of the ladder. Without empathy, people will resist and I won't be able to accomplish the goals.

'For me, the key to developing empathy has been mindfulness. Before getting into mindfulness work I had no idea how to develop self-awareness. But mindfulness taught me simple breathing exercises that allowed me to become more aware of my body and senses, which provided the pathway to even greater self-awareness. So any time I feel tense, like I'm entering a zone in which I could start losing self-management, I tune in to my breath and it calms me down. I always come back to that in my leadership.'

There is good reason why the English language associates wisdom and connection with the word 'sense'. Consider, for example, *sensational, sensitive, sensible, common sense, makes sense*. Conversely, our language associates an absentminded life with disconnection from the senses—think *senseless, insensitive* and *nonsense*. I have yet to meet someone who wants to live a senseless life, yet this is exactly what an absentminded life is.

The body: the gateway to 'self'-awareness

When we sense the 'self' in self-awareness, the first and most obvious aspect of ourselves is our body. This too is a critical part of the first foundation of mindfulness. When we tune in to our bodies we are primarily engaging our sense of touch. This is why breath (touch) and the body scan meditation are such a big deal in all mature mindfulness teaching—they are a sense practice that allows us to tune in to the most obvious and easily experienced part of our selves, our body.

In the west we generally believe our minds are separate from and superior to our bodies. But as neuroscientist Dr John Montgomery explains, the mind and the body have an intimate, inseparable relationship. Without the body, we would have no functional mind. The brain, he suggests, houses topographic body 'maps' that can respond to and activate every part of the body. Our bodies can be stimulated not only by real experiences, but also by simply thinking of experiences. We make decisions based on how they feel in the body. 'It seems that we can never race away in our thoughts without taking the body with us,' he writes, 'because our bodies are, in effect, always *part of* our thoughts. But we can certainly become, to varying degrees, 'disconnected' from, or consciously unaware of, our bodies … Without full awareness of our bodies, we're never really sure what we feel. And since our feelings are designed to tell us what is most important to us—what really *means* something to us—when we disconnect from our bodies and our feelings, we can lose a sense of meaning in our lives. We can find ourselves focusing on things that, in truth, hold little real value for us.'[2]

I stress this because 'tuning in to our bodies and senses' sounds so simplistic and insignificant, but it is in fact a very big deal. It is the gateway to full awareness.

The four foundations of mindfulness

You can be mindful of everything you perceive, think, know, intuit and experience (which is vast), but in developing mindfulness it can be very helpful to orient your practice around four foundations, each with its own nuances, lessons and insights.[3] These are:

1. **Mindfulness of the body/senses:** As already described, this foundation is the easiest and least subtle aspect of self-awareness, which is why most mindfulness training, especially in beginner programs, is so focused on mindfulness of breathing and the body. This foundation includes being mindful of the physical world. That is, it's about being present both to your internal body sensations and to external components, such as truly listening to people, watching the road when driving your car and tasting your food as you eat.

2. **Mindfulness of feeling tone:** Mindfulness allows us to notice our reactions to physical sensations and their accompanying emotions and to gain an understanding of our relationship with our inner and outer world. Becoming mindful of the feeling tone helps us to see our preferences in the world and within ourselves (chocolate over strawberry ice cream, joyful feelings over heavy dull feelings). Our experience of *pleasant*, *unpleasant* or *neutral* may appear to be inherent to the thing we contact, but on closer examination it actually depends on the *process* of contact. We are involved. The biggest insight from paying attention here is to notice our reactions when we encounter unpleasant, pleasant or neutral. We naturally seek to avoid the unpleasant, crave and cling to the pleasant, and generally ignore the neutral. Tuning in to our default reactions mindfully is a fundamental aspect of interrupting our conditioned responses to our experiences, and of developing inner strength, empathy and connectedness. Learning to stop running away from uncomfortable emotions through numbing, repressing or acting out is a critical element of integrity and maturity. We will explore this in forthcoming chapters.

3. **Mindfulness of thoughts:** When we are unmindful, we associate and identify ourselves with our thoughts. We become entranced by our own minds and believe our thoughts represent objective truths (even though the vast majority are based on subjective assumptions and imagination). If our thinking is challenged by others, we feel personally challenged and quickly move to defend or rationalise our position, which damages our leadership credibility. Mindfulness helps us to become more objective, less attached and more rational in our thinking. Critically, it releases us from huge doses of self-judgement and opens the way for kindness, curiosity and learning. When we are no longer invested in defending our thoughts or ideas, we are able to truly test our ways of thinking and discover new ways of thinking.

4. **Mindfulness of the way we make meaning:** The interpretations we make and conclusions we draw from life experiences and about what things mean are based on fundamental assumptions. Not only do we usually not question these assumptions, but we're often not even aware of them. The fourth foundation is being aware of the broader framework from which we derive meaning about what's going on, and therefore draw the conclusions we do. It's being awake to the lessons we learn and the interpretations, prejudices and values underlying those lessons. It's being mindful of our deeply held views, set ideas and unconscious biases—the ways we filter reality. Mindfulness allows us to see through our fixed views, to let go of old prejudices and unhelpful, embedded beliefs (such as 'I am not good enough').

Once we become mindful of these four foundations, we are no longer possessed by them or pushed around helplessly by them. Mindfulness is the key to liberating ourselves from the incessant push and pull of our physical sensations, emotions and thoughts. But in order to become truly useful and effective, mindfulness must be extended over time. It's not enough just to touch the present every now and then;

we must be present continuously for long periods of time. When we are, we start noticing our self-defeating habitual patterns of thought, feeling and behaviour through the lens of objective mindfulness. Thus we are able to start stepping free of them.

Transforming ourselves through self-awareness

Mindfulness answers the practical question of how to develop self-awareness. The only way you can become self-aware in real time is to be aware of your body, your feelings and emotions, your thoughts and your deeply held views. There is nothing else you can be 'self-aware' of. When we develop an authentic mindfulness practice, we implicitly build our self-awareness. Without mindfulness, it's impossible to develop enough self-awareness to genuinely transform our behaviour. The four foundations of mindfulness, then, are the practical application of self-awareness. If someone were to instruct you to 'be self-aware right now', you would first need to tune in to one of the foundations.

To illustrate how the four foundations of mindfulness can be applied in the context of self-awareness and transformation, I'll share a personal story.

I used to judge people quite a lot, especially silently in my mind. After being told how damaging this habit was, I decided to practise mindfulness to do something about it.

1. Becoming mindful of my body, I noticed when I was having critical thoughts. I felt tense, sometimes even mildly nauseated. Mindfulness of the body usually gives us the first clue we are up to something that is increasing our suffering (and often that of others).

2. When I started being mindful of my body, I noticed a pervasive emotion of anger. The feeling tone of anger is unpleasant. I noticed my reaction to this unpleasant emotion

was aversion. I used to idealise myself (delusionally) as a totally anger-free person. Whereas previously I would push my angry emotions away in a desperate attempt to keep my precious self-image intact, I was now able to be honest with myself and own up to my anger.

3. I finally became aware of the critical thoughts that accompanied the emotion of anger. I examined them objectively, as if they were not mine, without blaming or judging myself. I stopped buying into them and engaging with them as if they were objective truth.

4. On deeper investigation (another quality of mindfulness), I was able to recognise the unexamined assumption behind my critical thoughts. My assumption was that by criticising others I would feel superior and more worthy of connection and love. You can no doubt see the irony, but this is the sort of irrational thinking by which we live when we are not mindful. We engage in unexamined thoughts and behaviours that are truly unhelpful to ourselves and others.

After really seeing this in the bright light of mindfulness the habit began to dissolve.

Stages of mindfulness development

My first mentor shared a personal story to teach me how mindfulness can develop in stages over time. He used to drive an old Rolls-Royce with roll-down windows. When someone would cut in front of him he would roll his window down, stick his head out, yell a few choice words at the other driver and make a rude hand signal. One day this happened when he was driving with his elderly mother. When he pulled back inside and rolled the window up his mother said, 'I wish you would stop that. You're embarrassing me.' He immediately started arguing with her, rationalising and defending his behaviour, until she finally insisted that he just take her home.

The next few times he drove the same thing happened. It took him a while before he finally started becoming mindful of the habit. He worked through the following four stages toward overcoming it:

- **Stage 1: No real mindfulness.** Initially he had no awareness and therefore no accountability for his actions.

- **Stage 2: Mindfulness too late.** He started noticing what happened after he rolled his window back up. 'Oops,' he would think, 'I've done it again.' There hasn't yet been any real behaviour change, but there has definitely been progress. It takes a lot of courage to continue going at this point, especially since we tend to shame ourselves a lot here.

- **Stage 3: Mindful of the impulse.** The next time someone cut him off, he recognised his body's urge to react. He would feel the itch to move his hand and reach for the handle. His heart rate would rise. On one occasion, he didn't become aware until he felt the breeze on his face as he began to stick his head out the window. Mindful of the physical impulse, he was able to catch himself. This is why mindfulness of the body is so critical. It interrupts our reactive behaviour and gives us our best selves.

- **Stage 4: Dissolution of the impulse and habit.** Through mindfulness over time, he was able to conquer the self-defeating habit. Mindfulness can take us all the way into complete freedom. We may still have traces of repeat offending, but they are increasingly rare as our mindfulness grows.

The research on mindfulness

It's interesting to note the surge in mindfulness research over the past few years. The first decade of the twenty-first century in particular has seen exponential growth in the number of studies on the subject.[4] In 2003, 53 papers were published in scientific journals on mindfulness; by 2012, that number had jumped to 477.[5]

One of the more fascinating discoveries on mindfulness has been in the field of cognitive neuroscience, where research has found it can literally change the structure and function of the brain:

- **at the cellular level.** Meditation has been proved to change our brain chemistry by increasing the production of neurotransmitters and hormones associated with positive mood and feelings of relaxation and happiness.[6] The practice of meditation has also been shown to decrease concentrations of stress hormones[7] and boost immune system function[8].

- **at the structural level.** The practice of mindful meditation changes the structure of no fewer than eight regions of the brain.[9] In the cortical regions of the brain, the home of cognition and executive function, researchers have demonstrated that meditation increases the volume and density of grey matter[10] (neurons) as well as the density of white matter[11] (axons) that connect specific regions of the brain. These findings provide substantial evidence that meditation effectively 'rewires' the brain through the process of neuroplasticity.[12]

- **at the functional level.** The practice of meditation changes the pattern of electrical activity (neurons firing) observed in the brain.[13] Functionally speaking, this observation helps to explain the increases in self-awareness, attention control and emotional regulation that result after even brief periods of mindful meditation training.[14]

Taken together these findings provide concrete evidence that mindful meditation training leads not only to subjective improvements in wellbeing, but to changes in the brain at the cellular, structural and functional levels. Mindful meditation triggers more than a placebo effect. There is a cause-and-effect relationship between the practice of meditation and neuroplastic changes in the brain that lead to improvements in depressive symptoms, feelings of happiness and executive function.

Hundreds of research studies have indicated that mindfulness practice can provide the following additional benefits:

- **Stress and anxiety reduction:** More than 160 studies have shown mindfulness practice to have a positive and substantial effect on factors of wellbeing, including reducing stress, negative mood and anxiety.[15] One study on mindfulness practice in the workplace found a 36 per cent decrease in stress levels.[16]

- **Improved cognitive skills:** Mindfulness practice leads to significant improvements in critical cognitive skills after only four days of training for 20 minutes a day, including sustained attention, visuospatial processing and working memory, which helps with processing and reasoning.[17] It also improves our ability to focus attention and suppress distracting information, as well as increasing our information processing speed.[18] Mindfulness has been proven to create structural and functional changes in the brain such as generation of new brain cells (neurogenesis), particularly in the memory and executive functioning centres, dementia prevention and reduced activity in the amygdala (responsible for fear generation and 'fight or flight' reactions).[19]

- **Enhanced creativity:** Mindfulness practice can reduce 'cognitive rigidity', thus enabling us to respond with greater flexibility to situations in which we might otherwise be blinded by past experience.[20]

- **Stronger relationships:** Mindfulness has been shown to reduce social anxiety, improve our ability to communicate our feelings, increase empathy and decrease emotional reactivity.[21]

- **Increased compassion:** In one study, people who practised mindfulness-based meditation over just eight weeks displayed a 50 per cent increase in compassionate behaviours in real-life settings compared with those who did not meditate.[22]

- **Spiritual benefits:** Mindfulness has been shown to enhance self-insight, morality, intuition and fear modulation.[23]

- **Health benefits:** Mindfulness also provides a number of health benefits, including depression prevention, increased immune functioning, pain control, improved sleep patterns, greater ability to curb and overcome addictions and binge eating, and improved heart health.[24]

Clearly, mindfulness practice can have a profound effect on one's ability to live a fuller, richer, more fulfilling life—and to lead effectively.

Formal and informal mindfulness practice

Mindfulness can be practised both formally and informally. Formal practice is typically sustained meditation. It's setting aside a specific time to sit, lie or stand silently in mindful awareness. Formal meditation can also be performed while walking slowly and being mindfully aware of our walking and breathing.

Informal practice is simply maintaining awareness in the present as we go through our daily activities. For example, you can practise informal mindfulness by consciously choosing to be present during a work meeting. Or you can choose to put away your smartphone and enjoy a meal with no interruptions or thoughts of past or future.

Both forms of mindfulness are equally important, and they support each other. Sustained formal practice gives us profound insights into our motivations, fears and delusions. It helps us to develop a deep understanding of our true nature. It helps us to identify and come to terms with our deepest wounds and to develop a caring and compassionate attitude toward ourselves and others. It also helps us to cultivate the habit of mindfulness. Informal practice sustains our awareness in our daily activities. It drives home the importance of staying present and supports the development of the habit of mindfulness through all aspects of our life. As Andrew Weiss, the author of *Beginning Mindfulness*, explains, 'Without informal practice, we would become schizophrenic, with one, deeper level of awareness when we are doing sitting or walking meditation and with another, less open level of awareness everywhere else.'

As we progress through this book, I will introduce a number of formal and informal mindfulness practices that are especially relevant to researched leadership behaviours. I'll teach you how to tune in to the present moment regardless of what is happening in your external world—especially when challenges are great and stress is high.

Mindfulness is a value proposition

You won't choose to be present with any consistency unless you see it as a superior value proposition to your habitual dwelling on the future and the past or just pleasantly zoning out. Being present is as much about deliberate focusing as it is about becoming disenchanted with endless thoughts and their false promise of security, approval and resolution of unfinished business.

My clients are extremely intelligent high achievers. They are trained to analyse the 'business case'.

> This has been one of my favourite elements of teaching mindfulness to business people—the need for disciplined clarity, free of jargon or assumption. And time and time again they have discovered that in practice mindfulness is a vastly superior value proposition. It delivers mental acuity, emotional intelligence, wellbeing, inner ease, creativity and connection.

Giving up your indulgence in thoughts can be a little like giving up your favourite chocolate addiction—you can feel less happy initially. But over time you will start enjoying the improved mental and emotional health that the consistent commitment to being present in your current activity or experience gives.

Let's continue now to learn how mindfulness can impact and improve the behaviours required for extraordinary leadership.

Chapter 2

Take 200 per cent accountability

As long as a man stands in his own way, everything seems to be in his way.
Ralph Waldo Emerson

The story is told in ancient Buddhist literature of a pampered princess who was walking barefoot in her father's kingdom when she stepped on a thorn. In pain, she demanded of her father's advisers that the entire kingdom be carpeted. One adviser made her a pair of sandals and kindly encouraged her to wear them instead of carpeting the kingdom.

This simple story reveals a mentality that we all engage in to one extent or another. We yearn for a world of soft carpet and no thorns. We operate under the unexamined belief that our conditions need to be okay for us to be okay. And in this belief, our mindfulness and our happiness become as fragile as a princess's delicate feet.

This mindset is also at odds with the accountability needed for great leadership. Our 'carpet' becomes our team, our customers, our boss, the economy, and we avoid facing ourselves. We fail to put on the sandals of accountability. 'I'll start leading more effectively when x changes,' x very rarely being the individual themselves.

In the past few years my team and I have had the privilege of guiding thousands of leaders through live leadership feedback sessions with their team. The feedback is about their leadership, not the team's performance. We also use a 360-degree report to support the feedback process.

Fascinatingly, about 90 per cent of the leaders we work with immediately start rationalising and defending their weak spots. 'I only micromanage the team because they are not delivering quality work!' Or, 'I know the team might think I don't hold people accountable for poor performance, but that's because I care so much about being kind to people.'

Sometimes I jokingly (and kindly) sum it up for them.

'Okay, so are you saying that your behaviour is justifiable in all circumstances and you have nothing to work on in yourself?'

They usually backtrack pretty quickly at this point.

'No, of course not.'

But astonishingly, within minutes they are back to rationalisation. One CEO we worked with even asked for a quota of rationalisations in his session, because opening up and really listening and self-reflecting was proving to be very challenging for him.

Let's face it, opening up to tough feedback is challenging for us all. Taking full accountability for our actions is confronting. I remember when I went through this same session with my own team. I felt pretty bruised afterwards, but it was an enormous turning point in my own leadership. And the absolute, fundamental key was being willing to stop the rationalisation and blaming and start getting real with myself.

Looking deeper

Positive psychologist Shawn Achor is one of the world's leading experts on the connection between happiness and success. He concludes from research: 'In reality if I knew everything about your external world, I can only predict 10 percent of your long-term happiness. 90 percent of long-term happiness is predicted by how your brain processes the world.'[1] It is only by mindfully taking accountability for our mindset and responses to circumstances that we can change our lives and improve our leadership.

That said, we might be forgiven for the mistaken view that our external world is causing us pain—it sure looks that way much of the time!

For example, consider two people stuck in traffic on their way to work. Both of them will be late unless the traffic eases up, yet neither of them has any urgent meeting to get to. Their external world is very similar. One of them is calm and relaxed, knowing full well that getting stressed won't make the traffic go faster, nor will it serve his wellbeing. The second is frustrated, angry and stressed. He's honking his horn, anxiously checking his watch every couple of minutes, cursing other drivers.

The stressed person is caught in the assumption that the traffic is the cause of his stress. And in an odd way, without looking deeper, there is logic to this thinking—but it's not the whole story. If our external world were the actual cause of stress, it would create stress for everyone in equal measure. Yet in this example the cause is clearly not external but within us. Sure, the external world provides plenty of triggers, but the ultimate cause is the way we internally process our external world.

In the light of cool reason, we can see this truth, but as my late father used to say, 'Shooting at a target is easy. But when bullets are flying back at you, it changes the game dramatically.' And it's when the bullets start flying back that we usually come undone and lose our mindfulness.

It's also important to understand that the 'bullets' are more than the challenge of present circumstances. Our behaviours are often triggered by conditioning embedded deep within our subconscious mind, often caused by painful or confusing childhood experiences.

According to Harvard professor Gerald Zaltman, 95 per cent of our thoughts, emotions and learning occurs without our conscious awareness. Most cognitive neuroscientists concur, with some putting the figure as high as 99.999 per cent. Dan Ariely, professor of psychology and behavioural economics at Duke University and author of *Predictably Irrational: The Hidden Forces that Shape our Decisions*, concludes from years of empirical research that 'we are pawns in a game whose forces we largely fail to comprehend'. David Eagleman, neuroscientist at Baylor College of Medicine and author of *Incognito: The Secret Lives of the Brain*, adds, '[C]onsciousness is the smallest player in the operations of the brain. Our brains run mostly on autopilot, and the conscious mind has little access to the giant and mysterious factory that runs below it.'

In other words, it's easy to acknowledge rationally and intellectually that our stress and suffering are caused by our mindset. But in practice, it is often triggered in ways we don't even understand. For example, I once worked with a client, a senior banking executive, who was told that he had to change or he was going to lose his job. I was hired as his coach. The behaviours threatening his job were that he always had to be right and he shamed and belittled people harshly and regularly. His attacks would be particularly vicious any time he felt threatened in a situation where his ideas might be disproved or he risked losing an argument.

After some inquiry-based mindfulness work we found the true cause of his destructive behaviour, the pattern running beneath the surface of his conscious awareness. In one session he confessed to me, through tears, that as a child his dad beat him regularly and belittled him cruelly. He also said that when he cried his dad would intensify the beatings and shaming. So he built defence mechanisms to protect himself from feeling vulnerable and powerless.

As an adult leader, this showed up as a need to always be right and to always have the last word on everything. In a misguided though understandable effort to protect himself from those old wounds, he was always sure to be in control, to put others down before they could put him down, to be closed off and invulnerable. His mind became stuck in a subconscious defence pattern and this pattern kept playing itself out in inappropriate ways. His career was burning down as a result.

It should be noted that some external factors will have a universal effect. For example, most, if not all, of us will be stressed if we don't have enough to eat or we are being physically threatened. To say that in these circumstances our stress is caused by our mindset is absurd. Here there is a *genuine* threat, and an activation or stress response is natural. Most of the time, however, stress is created through our unexamined conditioning and mindset.

Response-able leadership

Given how easy it is to slip into conditioned patterns and to be triggered by subconscious wounds from the past, we can see how critical mindfulness practice is, particularly in leadership. It's when we are leading that we usually face the greatest tests and the most pressure to perform. And it's under this pressure that we can all too easily slide into reactive patterns. We end up being a prisoner of our own thinking, wishing that our team or organisation was 'carpeted' rather than that we 'put on sandals'.

Meri Rosich, CEO of the marketing consulting firm App Strategy Labs in Singapore, shared an experience with me where she took accountability and 'put on sandals'. Earlier in her career, a large organisation where she worked underwent massive change in a short period of time. Senior executives were being replaced quickly, budgets were disappearing, hiring was frozen.

Meri had a subscription to a service that delivered audio recordings on mindfulness. She would listen to these every day on her way to work. One day the audio reminded her that you can't control what happens in your external world, but if you are mindful, you can control how you react to what happens. 'It was such a "wow" moment,' she recalled, 'to realise that I had complete choice over how I reacted to the situation. Up until then I was shut down into a defensive position. And at that point I realised that it doesn't matter what's out there. I'm just going to get my projects done. I'm going to do the best that I can for the team. But I want to be able to look back and feel really proud of this, and not be part of the problem but part of the solution. I'll try to change the culture if I have a chance, I'll try to implement workplace improvement policies. I realised that there is far more to life than these temporary circumstances, no matter how stressful they feel in the moment.'

Meri's example shows the empowerment that can result when we take responsibility for our mindset and experience. Taking responsibility is about empowering ourselves to become the captain of our own ship and our behaviour choices.

This is the essence of mindful leadership: recognising that reality is as it is, and no amount of anger, frustration or argument will help us deal with it constructively or compassionately. Or, as the late leadership guru Stephen R. Covey said, 'As long as you think the problem is out there, that very thought is the problem.'

Viktor Frankl provides a wonderful example of mindfulness in the most extreme circumstances. A Jewish psychiatrist, in 1944 Viktor was transported by the Nazis from the Theresienstadt ghetto to the infamous Auschwitz concentration camp, and later to Dachau. Shortly after his release he published his book *Man's Search for Meaning*, which is recognised as one of the most influential books in history. Frankl famously wrote, 'We who lived in concentration camps can remember the men who walked through the huts comforting others, giving away their last piece of bread ... they offer sufficient proof that everything can be taken away from a man but one thing: the last of the human freedoms—to choose one's attitude in any given set of circumstances, to choose one's own way.'

In a global study that was repeated five times, leadership experts Jim Kouzes and Barry Posner found that one of the top four qualities we want in leaders is 'inspiring'.

> *What can be more inspiring than seeing a human being choose responsibility, compassion and generosity in the face of challenge? The best leaders inspire us to become better people through their own example. This is the primary role of leadership, as well as a core ethos of mindfulness.*

Liberating your leadership potential

Stuart Holmes, the managing director of specialist visual technologies company, PSCO Ltd in the UK, shared with me how mindfulness enabled him to take responsibility, and the effect it had on his leadership. When he first started the business as a young man, his biggest challenge was to try to solve every problem himself before his employees had the chance to sort things on their own. This is a very common reaction that many business owners experience, and it can be a lengthy learning process to work out where the boundaries are so that team members don't feel undermined and undervalued.

Stuart spent a lot of time and energy trying to fix the business and improve processes. He fell into the trap of thinking all his problems were external to himself and that his own mindset and behaviour had nothing to do with the limitations they kept hitting as a business. He was working longer hours and harder than anyone else, and getting increasingly frustrated with a lack of results and a lack of performance in his team. All he knew how to do was to work harder, which made him even more frustrated.

Thankfully, Stuart found a mentor, Jon Treanor, who introduced him to mindfulness. He started self-reflecting in a way he never had before, which allowed him to see that he was not leading effectively—that, in fact, the problem was *him*. After working with Jon, he said, 'My energy changed very quickly. Empathy and understanding began to creep in that wasn't there before. I realised my staff were not supposed to be mini-me's and I had failed to really see them, connect with them and support their needs. No wonder they were not performing like me!

'The key was learning to be honest with myself. I was blaming everyone else for why we were stuck. But mindfulness helped me see that the only way I could solve our problems was to change the way I worked. Now the first thing I look at is what I need to change in myself. I look at how I'm going to interact with people to ensure they understand the importance of what I'm asking them to do. And it's my responsibility to make sure they are empowered with the right resources, understanding and support. This has changed our whole business.'

Stuart is not alone in improving his business by becoming self-aware and taking personal accountability. According to research by Korn Ferry, the world's largest executive search firm, there is a direct correlation between leaders' self-awareness and profitability. The company analysed almost 7000 self-assessments from professionals at 486 publicly traded companies to identify the 'blind spots' in individuals' leadership characteristics. A blind spot is defined as a skill the professional counts among their strengths, when co-workers see that same skill as one of the professional's weaknesses. The analysis demonstrated that, on average, in poor-performing companies professionals:

- had 20 per cent more blind spots than those working at financially strong companies
- were 79 per cent more likely to have low overall self-awareness than those at firms with strong rates of return.

Joy Hazucha, global vice-president of the Korn Ferry Institute, commented, 'Self-awareness can directly translate into better choices and results in more fulfilling careers. On the other hand, those with low self-awareness tend to scramble the messages they receive concerning improvement, interpreting them as a threat rather than an opportunity.'

Leaders like Stuart who cultivate the courage to take an honest look at themselves find that taking accountability can have far greater impact on their business than any strategy, initiative or marketing campaign.

Accountability is a core mindfulness practice

Think of the leader who buys into the idea that stress is caused by others all day and then puts on their favourite meditation track in the evening to 'relieve' the day's stress. As I write this I remember one of my mindfulness teachers saying, 'This is not a skilful understanding of mindfulness at all.'

Mindfulness was never taught only for meditation purposes. It was always meant to be an integrated practice and, critically, a practice that cuts through the thinking that creates and supports suffering. When we fail to take accountability and to self-reflect we cause ourselves more stress and suffering, even despair. We believe there is no way out of our stress except for the external world to change, yet we also know deep down that we have no control over it. In fact, this is one of our greatest sources of stress. It leaves us in a constant state of low-grade anxiety.

We find solutions and relief only as we turn inward. As the Dalai Lama said, 'When you think everything is someone else's fault, you will suffer a lot. When you realize that everything springs only from yourself, you will learn both peace and joy.' We discover a profound strength and comfort in the truth that the answer to every problem lies within us in the present moment.

> *Mindfulness gives us both the insight to recognise that we are accountable and the tools for shifting into a new way of being, behaving and seeing the world that reduces our suffering and that of others.*

It's the frustrated person in the traffic who truly and honestly sees that they can choose a different response to the traffic, that they have real choice over their actions. As a beginning, they can focus on their breath and calm down their frazzled system so their brain regains executive function and they can respond more reasonably. It's the leader who quits blaming others for team issues and starts getting truly honest with themselves and begins to change their behaviour first, and in doing so inspires others to do the same.

Campbell McGlynn, HR Director at IRT, a hospital and healthcare firm in Australia, shared with me, 'Before mindfulness training I struggled to accept the role I had played in bad situations. But now, when things go wrong, I'm really quite comfortable asking myself, "What could I have done differently?" Mindfulness has given me a greater level of self-awareness, which enables me to more reflectively understand cause and effect, and to see my responsibility in all situations.'

Credibility-killer, life-stealer

The thinking and behaviours we engage in when not taking accountability for our actions typically take one or more of these forms:

- rationalisation
- defensiveness
- denial
- aggressiveness
- blame
- isolation (running away)
- stonewalling
- passive–aggressive retreat/withdrawal
- the PR spin (for example, we are told we are not delegating well, but rather than changing we 'sell' ourselves by pointing out how excellent our results are)
- deflection (the politician's favourite).

Intellectually, it makes absolutely no sense to engage in these behaviours. We lose credibility, arrest our learning and growth, and become rigid and narrow. I have personally witnessed these behaviours end careers and cost companies millions of dollars. So the question is, *why*? Why would we sooner engage in convincing ourselves and others we are right, rather than looking within and reaping the rewards of a deeper integrity both within ourselves and with others?

As in many areas of mindfulness practice, we need to look deeper. We need to pay attention more closely to what is happening when we are rationalising. The primary payoff we get for rationalising and blaming is a sense of security and emotional comfort. If we could slow time, we would notice that when we receive uncomfortable feedback and then engage in defensiveness, rationalisation, aggressiveness or blame, we win a temporary reprieve from feelings of vulnerability and discomfort. In fact, we engage in what some would term 'insane' behaviours for a very sane reason: to gain a sense of security, an easing of our distress and a return to equilibrium. Food, TV, drugs and alcohol can offer the same temporary relief. And, like all of these props, the net result is numbness.

While numbness is much more attractive than discomfort or fear or insecurity, it is a life-stealer. As research professor and best-selling author Brené Brown puts it, 'We cannot selectively numb emotions. When we numb the painful emotions, we also numb the positive emotions.' And that means we are less present in our lives and less available to experience the wonderful emotions like joy and deep fulfilment. Our life narrows and we are so much the poorer for it.

Distress intolerance and equanimity

Our desire to avoid uncomfortable feelings is referred to by psychologists as 'distress intolerance', which is defined as the 'perceived inability to fully experience unpleasant, aversive or uncomfortable emotions, and is accompanied by a desperate need to escape the uncomfortable emotions'.[2]

None of us like experiencing unpleasant emotions. But there's a difference between disliking them while accepting they are an inevitable part of life, and experiencing them as unbearable and desperately trying to avoid and rid ourselves of them.

If we can't stick with the distress, breathing through it and into it, we have no chance of developing a deeper level of mindfulness and ease in our lives. The journey to mental and emotional strength, healing and wholeness is through embracing our whole lives and our whole selves, warts and all. This is the heart of an authentic life and authentic leadership. We cannot heal until we learn to sit with our sadness, pain and insecurity. Ironically, we can even run from the intensity of our deepest joy, love and sense of peace; they too can be overwhelming. Our ability to feel true bliss is proportionate to our willingness to face difficult feelings.

Kevin Pickhardt, the CEO of Pharos, teaches everyone in his company the mindfulness principle of moving toward difficult emotions, particularly anger and fear, rather than running from them. 'Anger and fear are not something to try to eliminate,' he suggested to me. 'They are something to embrace. They are there to teach us, to awaken us and get us to pay attention to something. When we feel those feelings, something important is going on that we need to learn from. And we learn from them by recognising and living with discomfort—we learn to live with the void of "I don't know what's going to happen".'

While mindfulness practice re-sensitises us to our lives, it also helps us develop a critical quality for embracing our whole lives: equanimity, an inner steadiness and balance regardless of what is happening in our external world. My friend Patrick Kearney, a highly regarded teacher of mindfulness, shared with me that one of the great symbols of equanimity is the Daruma doll in Japan. These dolls are designed so that when they are knocked over, they always bounce back up again. Equanimity is like that—a steady upright place inside yourself that bounces back no matter what happens in your external world.

As Patrick said, 'If you're cultivating mindfulness, then you are paying continuous attention to whatever happens. You have to develop an attitude of acceptance of whatever happens. Otherwise, you can't do it. You may be mindful of one thing, but something else may be too difficult for you to handle. So you'll escape into thinking and distraction. But as your mindfulness practice matures, you learn to stay with whatever is going on, and this naturally develops into equanimity. As one of my teachers put it, it's "taking refuge in the present".'

Spencer Sherman, Founder and Executive Chairman of the financial planning firm Abacus Wealth Partners in the US, sees developing equanimity as one of the greatest benefits of mindfulness. 'For the leader of any organisation there are going to be storms,' he told me. 'If you're not cultivating some sense of equanimity within yourself, if you're not aware of how you're responding to the changing world, there's little hope of finding your centre and keeping everybody else centred through those storms. This is what makes a true leader: how are you when colleagues are disagreeing with you and revenues are declining? Mindfulness practice is no longer a luxury, but a necessity.'

Leaning in deeper

By cultivating our ability to tolerate our difficult feelings and stay open instead of contracting into defensiveness, we can discover so much more about ourselves. Our self-awareness can grow exponentially, and with it our capacity for transformation and real change. This is another gift of truly looking inward without defensiveness—the vulnerable path.

Earlier I gave the example of my banking executive client who discovered the deeply rooted childhood trauma that was dictating his self-destructive behaviours and threatening his job. Through mindfully leaning in, and not running from his distressing feelings of fear and vulnerability, he began to break the old patterns, the defence mechanisms designed to protect him. He learned to breathe through the triggers that arose when he felt challenged or criticised. He slowly became aware that it was okay to feel scared or vulnerable, and that he wouldn't be physically harmed or lose his job or lose respect. In fact, he discovered that as he allowed himself to be vulnerable, the opposite happened: he won greater respect—and he kept his job.

> *Mindfulness is not a process of selecting which aspects of life we want to deal with. It is the practice of embracing all of life, both the joy and the pain.*

By 'embracing' I mean being present, being honest and compassionate with ourselves and our experience, without negotiation or resistance.

This is the way to a truly wonderful life with so much less fear, angst and fixation. This is how we build our resilience, inner strength and equanimity, and therefore our overall wellbeing.

You can't do it without inner kindness

Accepting accountability for ourselves can be confronting on the best of days. If we follow up those moments of self-honesty with harsh self-judgement, it becomes a real struggle that leads to more suffering. In fact, 'taking accountability' can become a form of inner torment.

All too often we buy into the view that transformation comes from judgemental criticism or threat (we need to 'teach ourselves a lesson'). Criticism or threat can be directed inward toward ourselves and outward toward others. Unfortunately, in both cases it only increases the distress in our nervous system and, more often than not, leads to silent self-soothing in the form of rationalisation ('It was her fault anyway') or silent rebellion against our harsh inner critic ('To hell with it, I'll do what I like!').

Think of it this way: Would you like to work in a team where honest feedback was consistently delivered with an intention to shame, scare or belittle you or your co-workers into compliance? Do you believe deep trust and effectiveness would be nurtured by this culture? Yet if we are not mindful we tend to use this method on ourselves, which leads to a range of unmindful responses, including trying to earn others' approval, rebellion, self-centredness, numbness, denial, striving in stress and a deep sense of unease.

Mindful accountability involves neither attacking ourselves nor rationalising our behaviour. The key is being kind and compassionate toward ourselves. Kindness allows us to examine our behaviour with non-judgemental curiosity and honesty when we have acted poorly or violated our values. It helps us to bear the truth rather than ramping up our distress. In doing so it helps us to see the *why* behind such actions—and our underlying needs that are not being met. For example, our banking executive just wanted to feel accepted and safe. In getting really honest with himself in a kind and compassionate way, he could see this and start kinder relationships with himself and with others.

Kindness doesn't excuse or rationalise the behaviour. The goal is still to keep correcting course and realigning with our best selves. But *how* we do that makes all the difference.

In his excellent book *Soul without Shame: A Guide to Liberating Yourself from the Inner Judge*, mindfulness teacher Byron Brown explains that we all have an inner judge, which he defines as 'the force in you that constantly evaluates and assesses your worth as a human being and thus limits your capacity to be fully alive in the present moment'. In other words, it robs you of a deep, rich mindfulness.

The original function of the judge was to act as your conscience. It learned acceptable behavioural standards from parents and society, then used guilt and shame to keep you in line with those standards. The unfortunate side effect of keeping you 'socialised' and your behaviour 'acceptable' is that this also suppresses your natural creativity and openness. Maturing as an adult requires that you replace the judge with a 'living conscience' based on a recognition of your authentic, essential nature. Brown explained, 'Disengaging from the judge thus serves two functions: to free you from the confinement of old, limiting patterns and beliefs and, at the same time, to demand that you actively practice living in a way that eliminates the need for the judge. You cannot simply throw off a structure that has defined and supported you unless you have something more effective with which to replace it. You must learn to function, interact, and make choices freed from the standards of the judge, which means living in alignment with the truth and reality of your own life at the present time. This creates a living conscience that is not based on rules. Such a conscience allows the fullness of your living soul to express itself.'

In short, mindfulness allows us to be honest with ourselves and hold ourselves accountable with a 'living conscience' that is not judgemental or critical, but rather kind and compassionate.

True compassion is not a tool of self-deception, whereby we soothe ourselves with justifications. On the contrary, it's precisely what allows us to look at our behaviours with stark, objective honesty. It stops our conditioned defensiveness in its tracks because we're no longer attacking ourselves. And when we're not in defence mode, we can analyse and respond with more clarity and creativity. We're no longer reacting to harsh criticism, but rather responding to the call of authentic conscience.

When I teach leaders about the importance of self-kindness, I often encounter an interesting perspective. Many leaders resist casting off the inner judge because of a deeply rooted fear that if they stop attacking themselves, they will become apathetic and irresponsible. They feel that self-attack motivates them to continually improve and achieve. The only reason they get out of bed, keep striving and keep improving, so this thinking goes, is because their inner judge forces them to. They fear that if they let go of their inner judge, their life would disintegrate—they would become lazy and tune out.

The research suggests otherwise. From four separate experiments, researchers Juliana Breines and Serena Chen concluded that 'taking an accepting approach to personal failure may make people more motivated to improve themselves'. Among other benefits, self-compassion creates:

- greater belief that a personal weakness can be changed for the better
- greater motivation to make amends and avoid repeating a moral transgression
- greater motivation to change the weakness.[3]

Kindness is a form of mindfulness. It has an embracing quality, allowing us to see things as they really are, rather than through a lens of shame or denial.

Taking 200 per cent accountability

When I start a mindful accountability journey with leaders, it's not uncommon for them to recognise how they have been blaming others for a lack of results, but then to swing to the opposite end of the scale and take 100 per cent responsibility for *everything* that happens in their team or organisation. The truth is that the blame for dysfunction and poor performance can't be laid solely at the feet of either the leader or the team. Everyone shares responsibility, and everyone must take full accountability—but only for that which they control. The equation is 100 per cent from the leader plus 100 per cent from the team equals 200 per cent accountability.

A partnership in which one person takes full accountability and the other takes only partial accountability is dysfunctional. It simply doesn't work. If you hold yourself accountable without holding your partner accountable, you create a narcissist. The saying 'It takes two to tango' applies here. It takes two to cause dysfunction, but it also takes two to fix that dysfunction. And of course this principle applies to whole teams and organisations.

Organisational scientist Peter Senge puts it like this: 'Personal change and organizational change are always two sides of the same coin, and the fantasy we often carry around that somehow my organization will change without me changing is truly crazy.' If we don't acknowledge this two-way street to change we invariably buy into a 'Messiah Myth' in organisations, where one person saves the day all by themselves, or we communicate that others need to change, but not ourselves. The first option ensures no one looks at themselves for change and the second option will absolutely guarantee resistance to change. Neither option produces real or lasting transformation.

200 per cent in action

I once worked with a struggling CEO who became emotionally abusive when people did not meet his expectations, then angrily took their workload on himself. Ironically, he brought us in to help him develop real accountability and performance in his business. But he wanted us to change his people, change the system, change anything but himself. He could not see the links between his behaviour and the organisational outcomes. In fact, like so many leaders, he was not even aware that his behaviour was supporting the exact opposite of what he was trying to achieve.

We made an agreement based on the concept of 200 per cent accountability, meaning he was 100 per cent responsible for changing his self-sabotaging behaviour, while his team were 100 per cent responsible for delivering their outcomes. It was a contract of trust and responsibility, with clear consequences and accountability for change. Five years later, his team's revenue and profit have nearly doubled and he is no longer engaging in his self-sabotaging behaviour.

Deven Billimoria, an outstanding leader and the CEO of Smartgroup, an outsourced salary packaging service in Australia, shared a story with me about how mindfulness and 200 per cent accountability worked for him. As his company was going through a fast growth phase, Deven needed to take on a bigger role in the company, which required other executives to step in and fill the void as he relinquished some duties to take on others. Things were slipping through the cracks and weren't getting done. He was feeling exhausted, stressed and anxious, and he started behaving in disrespectful ways. As we all do at times, he lost his way behaviourally.

The turning point was when his team stepped up and told him they were unhappy with his behaviour. They didn't mind that he was holding people accountable, but they were unhappy with his style. As all the best leaders do, Deven self-reflected and took responsibility for his actions. He recognised the state of stress he was leading from and committed to re-commence his mindfulness meditation practice and re-centre himself.

A few weeks later he met with all his senior executives. They discussed the problems and came up with a solution that everyone contributed to and was happy with. Deven told me, 'The only reason we were able to even have those conversations is because I had pulled myself away and addressed my own dysfunction. If I had tried to say something earlier, when I was grumpy, irritable and anxiety-ridden all the time, it would have just seemed like I wasn't taking accountability for my actions. And that would have been the case—I would have just been blaming others for not stepping up. I was in a reactive state. But once I was able to get that calmness of mind, then I was able to take accountability for my own actions first, and then hold my team accountable in a kind, calm and patient way. When I approached the team, it came from a loving, inspirational place, not a reactive, anxiety-driven place. Mindfulness makes all the difference in my ability to deal with frustrating situations appropriately and to hold myself and everyone else accountable without making anyone feel shamed or belittled.'

Deven's story reminded me of a time when I confessed to a client that I had been acting dysfunctionally with my own team and that I was busy course-correcting myself. He looked at me in shock and said, 'Hang on a minute. You've been practising mindfulness for decades. Surely you should have eliminated your dysfunction a long time ago and learned how to always be impeccable?'

I remember laughing hard. 'No,' I replied, 'that would be seriously delusional.'

Yes, with mindfulness we slowly but surely move toward consistently healthy behaviour. But there will always be blind spots and challenges. The real gift of ownership and mindfulness is that it allows us to correct course so much faster. It keeps us humble and real. Above all, mindfulness teaches us that we are fallible! And that is one of its greatest gifts. When we are mindful, we don't waste time and energy defending and rationalising our actions. We take a good, undefended look and get on with re-engaging in the healthiest possible way, just as Deven did.

True freedom is available

Our life will never be free of challenges. The thorns will always be there. But with mindfulness, challenges never seem so big they threaten to overwhelm us. We can access that calm centre and see our life and the problem in a broader context. From the perspective of brain science, we can maintain executive function in the face of the most difficult challenges.

Inevitably thorns will still penetrate our mindfulness sandals. It's really not a perfect process—we are human after all. This is another reason to be deeply kind and patient with ourselves on the journey toward full presence and accountability. There are more than enough thorns out there; we don't need to add our own.

The external world can never be completely satisfying. This is just the nature of reality. External conditions are just too unstable to provide any lasting solidity or security. No matter where we go or what we do, as long as we believe the world needs to be carpeted for us to feel secure, we will always carry this sense of dissatisfaction. Change and instability are in the nature of things.

The key difference between an authentic practitioner of mindfulness and those lost in mindlessness is that mindfulness practitioners relinquish the belief that external conditions can provide the peace, aliveness and security we all long for. As they wake up to this truth, their mind and heart settle and open to life as it is. And as this process unfolds they come to realise that mindfulness itself, the full embracing of life and being present to it regardless of conditions, is where true satisfaction lies.

We cannot inspire change in others until we learn to change ourselves. We cannot maintain presence, aliveness or credibility if we blame others or rationalise unmindful behaviour.

Taking accountability may seem like the hard path. But remember, it is easier to wear sandals than to cover the world with carpet. In this insight lies a great freedom, and a truly priceless gift for yourself and for those whom you connect with every day.

Chapter 3

Lead from mindful values

*Happiness is when what you think, what you say, and
what you do are in harmony.*

Mahatma Gandhi

If you've ever attended an insight mindfulness retreat, you will
have been asked to follow five basic values for the duration of
the retreat. Essentially, these values are (1) do no harm, (2) do
not steal, (3) abstain from any sexual conduct that will create either
distraction or pain, (4) always speak the truth, and (5) abstain from
intoxicants that may cloud or numb your consciousness.

Although I have attended many insight retreats I never took
these values seriously; in fact, I wrote them off as 'not applying
to me'. I have never been a fan of rules or strict guidelines for
behaviour, so while I had nothing against the spirit of the code I
just did not pay it much attention. It was only later in my practice
that I discovered the beauty of adhering to a code of wholesome,
life-serving values.

It first happened when I was attending a long retreat with the renowned mindfulness teacher Thich Nhat Hanh in France. As I was sitting with a friend, who was a monk in training, a mosquito landed on his arm. When the mosquito had sunk its long proboscis into my friend's arm, he started petting it with his finger. In my cynicism, I said, 'Oh my god, this is ridiculous. Give me a break!' It felt like this was taking the non-harming principle way too far.

My friend said something I'll never forget: 'Do you think mindful values are for the sake of the mosquito? If so, you're mistaken. The point of non-harming as a practice is about more than just honouring all life. It is to support your development of a wholesome, happy mind and heart. If you look more closely, with refined attention, can you notice what state your mind and heart are in when you are killing the mosquito? I humbly suggest to you that when we slap mosquitos, our frame of mind is fear and anger. And fear and anger, even to the slightest degree, create more suffering. Mindfulness practice is about freedom from suffering, is it not?'

I got it. A couple days later, a spider crawled onto my hand. Ordinarily, I would have flicked it off or just squashed it. But in this case, being mindful, I put my hand out and it crawled onto my finger. I placed it carefully on a plant. I was astonished to notice a deep love in my heart. The lesson sank in as I felt the essence of the mindfulness and care that cultivates healthy states of mind, along with a sense of happiness.

I realised then that wholesome values or principles are not about restrictions or harsh rules to follow. Rather, they are a wonderful container for the development of mindfulness. They give our mindfulness an easy reference point, an orientation to what wholesome and healthy looks like when we need it. In fact, they are an essential support for a happy, peaceful life. Mindfulness teaching does not focus on morality, but on what causes suffering and what alleviates it. It's not about guilt, punishment or rigid rules. It's an invitation to wholesomeness and wellness.

Why do values matter so much to leadership?

'Leadership,' write Jim Kouzes and Barry Posner, 'begins with a belief in yourself and continues only if other people believe in you.' To believe in you, people have to know (1) who you are and what you stand for, and (2) whether or not they can trust you. In other words, leaders must walk their talk, and in order to do that, they must have a talk to walk. Values are your talk, and living in accordance with them through your behaviour—what Jim and Barry call 'modelling the way'—is your walk.

Stephen Hickey, a partner at Aon Hewitt Australia and New Zealand, reports that the first shortcoming his organisation observes in leaders is when they 'don't lead by example or walk their own talk'. Research shows that this failing drastically affects engagement. When Jim and Barry asked people how effective they felt their leader was, their assessments clearly related to how frequently they observed that person 'model the way', or live according to their stated values. The most effective leaders model the way almost 47 per cent more often than their counterparts who were reported as least effective. Furthermore, people who report low engagement with their organisation reported that their leaders model the way nearly 36 per cent less often than leaders of people who were most engaged.

The beginning of your leadership journey is defining clearly who you are, what you stand for and what your deepest values are—in short, your leadership philosophy. In one research study by Jim and Barry, people who rated their leaders as 'almost always' clear about their leadership philosophy indicated trusting them 66 per cent more than those who said their leaders were 'almost never' clear. In other words, knowing your values and being able to articulate them is extraordinarily important for trust building, and without trust there is no leadership.

Tony Simons at Cornell University, author of *The Integrity Divide*, writes, 'Organizations where employees strongly believed their managers followed through on promises and commitments and demonstrated the values they preached were substantially more profitable than those whose managers scored average or lower.' Knowing and demonstrating your values is how you create trust among your team members, and trust is essential for organisational effectiveness.

One study investigated whether employees' perception of their manager's behavioural integrity influences job satisfaction, engagement, turnover, absenteeism, stress, work–family conflict, health and life satisfaction. The researchers found numerous correlations between perceived behavioural integrity and employee performance. Leaders with high perceived behavioural integrity lead teams that are significantly more satisfied in their job, less likely to be absent and less stressed, and that report greater overall health and wellbeing and life satisfaction. In short, 'good ethics make for good business'.[1]

What do we mean by 'values'?

Acceptance and commitment therapy (ACT) is a widely utilised, empirically based intervention that uses acceptance and mindfulness strategies to change behaviour and increase psychological flexibility. The therapy is based on the understanding that human meaning and purpose ultimately revolve around values. Values help people choose direction in their life that is congruent with what is deeply important to them and establish goals supporting movement in that direction. It is assumed here that we mean wholesome values — that is, values that when followed lead to more peace, happiness, vitality and wellbeing. The fundamental question ACT therapists ask their clients is, 'In a world where you could choose to have your life be about something, what would you choose?'[2]

ACT provides an excellent definition of values: 'Values are chosen concepts linked with patterns of action that provide a sense of meaning and that can coordinate our behavior over long time frames. Examples of such patterns might be acting lovingly toward one's partner or being present with one's children. Values in this sense can never be fulfilled, satisfied, or completed; rather, they serve to give us purpose or direction in each instance of behavior.'[3] In other words, values are essentially our personal code of conduct. They are the compass by which we determine our daily choices and actions.

Wholesome values matter more than you might imagine. To truly master living your values requires an extraordinary awareness, and a bone-deep honesty with yourself. But it is so very worth it. Living in alignment with wholesome values will bring you home to yourself. It will help you find a deep peace and ease with who you are and what you do in the world. As Gandhi put it so simply, it is happiness. It is no exaggeration to say that values support a deep level of discovery of what integrity means. And integrity, a sense of wholeness, is something we all long for.

Values for wellbeing

Living in accordance with our values is critical not only for leadership, but also for our own health and wellbeing. Many studies have confirmed this. One analysis of 63 different ACT-related studies showed that by helping clients choose wholesome values and align their behaviours with them, ACT effectively treats a variety of anxiety disorders. Consistently engaging in activities that align with wholesome values increases our psychological flexibility, which is the key to being open to experience and minimising our feelings of anxiety or worry.[4]

Another study showed that character-building exercises had a reliable positive effect on participants' wellbeing, academic self-efficacy and achievement. Expressing wholesome values reduces feelings of anxiety, and engaging in activities that build character increases our overall health and wellbeing.[5]

A similar study concluded, 'Character is not something you are born with, it is a skill that can be developed and improved over the course of your entire life.' Furthermore, character is a non-cognitive skill that better predicts both academic and workplace success when compared with measures of IQ. And it is a *learned skill*. All of us have the potential to improve our character, and thus our overall happiness and fulfilment, by aligning with our values.[6]

One team of researchers analysed the responses of 5299 individuals to identify how their scores on a Values in Action inventory of strengths related to life satisfaction. The higher a reported character strength, the higher the associated life satisfaction. Furthermore, the 'monotonic' effect of high character on life satisfaction means we cannot overdose on character. The stronger one's character, the more life satisfaction is felt.[7]

In a related study by Jim Kouzes and Barry Posner, managers were asked about their clarity around their personal values and the values of their organisation, and their level of commitment to their organisation. The results showed that being clear on your personal values is far more important than your organisation being clear on its values. This supports the ACT finding that living from your values leads to more vitality, and vitality shows up in more commitment to what you are doing. As a leader, defining and modelling shared values is critical. But first and most important is defining and modelling your personal values.

Living in accordance with our values, and with personal integrity, is about more than leading well. It's also about feeling happy with ourselves and our lives. Values give us personal clarity when those around us are being driven by fear, anxiety or other less-than-wholesome qualities.

Making a stand for something better

I often ask my clients to imagine the following scenario: In a playground of ten-year-olds a new kid from a different ethnic background is being abused by the school bullies, while the other kids stand by and watch. Which of the following courses would you want your child to choose?

1. Join in with the crowd and do nothing.

2. Join the bullies.

3. Stand up for the other child, for example by reporting the bullies or protecting the other child by fighting back.

Obviously, nearly everyone chooses option three. Granted, they choose it from the safety of a hypothetical. But they choose it for a reason: they know that is the wholesome values choice, while the other two are based on fear or ignorance. We all know that option three is the right choice—the *leadership* choice. It's that clarity of values and the conviction to live them under fire that builds and makes wholesome leaders. It allows the person to individuate under pressure, to be their own person, to be a leader.

Then I ask clients why they would want their child to choose option three when they will undoubtedly suffer for it by being beaten or bullied themselves, or deserted by and alienated from their timid friends. This is a fascinating discussion. Everyone knows in their heart that living wholesome values is a beautiful, worthwhile, meaningful endeavour that generates self-acceptance, strength and inner peace. The key, of course, is developing the awareness and strength not to be undermined by fear and greed, as the vast majority of people are when they feel their job, reputation or approval needs are threatened. We all love wholesome values, but we often lack the courage to live them because we have not come to appreciate how psychologically important they are for our wellbeing.

The best value to start with in leadership

Jim Kouzes and Barry Posner have surveyed well over 100 000 people to determine the personal traits, characteristics and attributes people look for and admire in leaders. Twenty distinct characteristics emerged from the answers to their open-ended questions. At the top of the list by a long way (89 per cent in 2012) is honesty. More than anything else, people want honesty from their leaders.[8] Yet leaders are failing miserably in this. The public relations firm Edelman publishes a global survey each year called the Trust Barometer, which gauges the public's trust in leaders and institutions. The 2014 survey, which analysed data from more than 33 000 respondents, found that only 20 per cent of people trust business leaders to tell the truth, and only 13 per cent trust government officials to tell the truth.[9] Edelman president and CEO Richard Edelman commented, 'We're clearly experiencing a crisis in leadership.'[10]

Please pause and think about this for a moment. Honesty is the quality we expect and value most from our leaders, yet it's the area where they seem to be failing the most. The data suggests that about four out of five leaders are in effect not leading anywhere near as effectively as they could and need to.

The question I've been asking for more than a decade is, 'How does one truly teach honesty to leaders who think they know, intellectually, exactly what it is but who in practice are falling short too often?' A first clue emerges when I share this research in seminars and ask participants if they think four out of five leaders know that they are distrusted. Do those leaders look in the mirror and admit to themselves that they are behaving in ways that alienate their team members? The overwhelming answer, of course, is no they don't.

Then I follow up with another question: 'So how can you be sure you are not doing exactly the same thing as them?' The audience goes quiet. If there is enough emotional safety in the room, many admit they actually don't know for sure. Our greatest challenge is not honesty with others (though that is tough too). Our greatest challenge is being honest with ourselves.

Meeting your shadow

The reason we're often unsure about how honest we are is because we have the capacity to hide parts of ourselves from ourselves. As Carl Jung, one of the fathers of modern psychology, explained, 'Everyone carries a shadow, and the less it is embodied in the individual's conscious life, the blacker and denser it is.' We are able to withhold uncomfortable truths from ourselves in the 'shadows' of our mind. This can often be explained by distress intolerance: if we cannot handle the discomfort of seeing certain truths about ourselves, we block them from ourselves and hide them in the shadows of our psyche.

Unfortunately, this creates the capacity for astonishingly hypocritical behaviours. For example, I was running a leadership training program for senior managers who reported to executive team members. During the training they declared, 'Our executives have no integrity.' A few days later, I discovered that the people beneath this group had exactly the same complaint. So they were self-righteously pointing at the lack of integrity of their bosses while engaging in the very same behaviour themselves. This is not unusual at all; in fact, it is the norm.

The human mind has a limitless capacity for self-deception. We hide our values violations from ourselves so skilfully that many times we are completely unconscious of when we have crossed a line. It's like we are playing a game of hide-and-seek with ourselves.

One of my least favourite parts of teaching this subject to groups is that they catch on really quickly and very easily see *my* shadow and hypocrisy when I am teaching. For example, one group let me know that I was clearly angry with them for being argumentative. How could I be angry and claim to be a mindfulness teacher? Every part of me wanted to deny it and run from the shame I felt at being exposed. Most importantly, I didn't want to admit it to myself. I had begun to believe my own PR that I was beyond that, more advanced than that. But once I had owned my shadow and admitted to it non-defensively, we were able to get back on track. I learned that it's okay to fail, that failure is our constant companion through life, and that it's not a great idea to deny the failure, especially when our credibility is on the line.

Mindfulness gives us the ability to 'make the unconscious conscious' by uncovering our shadow. We all seek peace and wholeness within ourselves, yet, as Jung concluded, as long as we are split from ourselves and deceive ourselves, this wholeness will elude us.

I have seen leader after leader not only improve their leadership, but also heal family relationships and their own life by 'owning their shadow' and getting honest with themselves. To use mindfulness language, they became willing to be fully awake and present to their darker side, their less pleasant thoughts and behaviours. And by doing so, they became progressively more liberated from them.

This is not standard corporate training, I know. But it is what is needed for true transformation. Without honestly addressing the investment we have in denial and rationalisation, all leadership and self-improvement efforts are more or less smoke and mirrors.

Values are the container for mindfulness

As important as values are to the practice of mindfulness, they are not mindfulness itself. If we could be perfectly mindful all the time, we would not really need to be reminded of values. We would be in tune with and consistently act from our most authentic, loving selves. The reality is that very few of us—perhaps none of us—are mindful all the time. Values give the mind and heart really important guidelines. They are a structure to orient our mindfulness. They serve as guideposts on our journey to reveal to us when we've strayed from the path. They are a container, a context for mindfulness.

Another analogy is to consider a finger pointing at the moon. Mindfulness is the moon; the pointing finger is values. Don't confuse the finger with the moon itself. Ultimately, wisdom and awareness are more important than values. However, values serve as a compass pointing the way.

We follow them not in order to look good or to win approval. It's not even that we 'should' follow values in order to be a good person. It's simply that they produce the states of mind that mindfulness produces: wholeness, wellness, trust, respect. They are a good reminder of what wholesome mindful action looks like—especially when we are not being particularly mindful.

Finding the courage to follow our values

Living according to our values is a process of maturation that takes courage. At times we may live values loosely but for the wrong reasons. We may comply with organisational values out of fear of losing our job. Or we may live them to appear good to others; in other words, it's not about the values themselves, but rather about protecting our image or position. Our understanding of values and our reasons for following them are largely externalised. The highest level of maturity involves internalising values and living them even at the expense of compliance or financial safety. We can know we really 'get it' when we live our values even, or especially, when it costs us dearly.

Delphine Wastiaux, Strategy and Incubation Manager at Veolia, an environmental services company in the UK, shared with me her personal journey through this process. After working in several positions under many different bosses within her company, she realised that she wanted to move up to an operational role. However, she struggled with her confidence because the profile of successful people in that role was very different from her personal style. She felt like her credibility was questioned, given that the typical profile was of a commanding, tough, direct style and she preferred a more collaborative approach. She felt pressure to copy the direct style in order to fit in.

After reflecting mindfully, she said, 'I realised I needed to take the good from that style while sticking to what I felt was important. I didn't need to completely reject the advice from people who had been here for a long time because they had valuable insights. But neither did I need to completely adopt everything they said. I could be true to myself without being defensive or hostile.' She got the job and has thrived there, making a significant contribution with her personal leadership style.

To return to the analogy of the carpet and the sandals, if our values integrity is based on external factors, then we're simply focusing on the carpet rather than putting on sandals. As long as the carpet is okay, we will follow our values. Maturing and internalising our values means putting on sandals and finding peace within ourselves by living wholesome values, regardless of what the carpet looks like.

I had a personal experience with this that I'll never forget. Shortly after the global financial crisis, my company was really struggling—in fact, close to bankruptcy. Then we signed on a new client, an iconic brand that put us back on the map. This was really our only chance of pulling out of dire straits.

It was during my second session working with the whole executive team that my values were put to the test. I'd spent only about three hours working personally with the CEO. We barely knew each other. In this session, he started verbally abusing one of his team members. It reached a point where I knew I was obliged to say something to stay true to my value of honesty. But I also knew the very existence of my company could be seriously threatened by my speaking out. In all likelihood, if it backfired on me, my business would tank. On the other hand, if I didn't say something, my values would be compromised.

I still remember vividly a bead of sweat trickling down my temple as I gently called him out on his behaviour. Thankfully, at heart he is a wonderful man and he took it well. He stopped himself and clarified what he was requesting. In the end, it created a great relationship between the two of us. I was deeply grateful that day not only because I kept the client and my business survived, but because I chose to live from my values whatever the consequences. I haven't always done this, and it's definitely still a work in progress, but when I do, I know with certainty that I'm on track.

When we base our wellbeing on external circumstances, a risk like this seems crazy and pointless. We don't really even understand the purpose of taking it. But when we truly integrate a values-based approach, we realise that if our fundamental identity and sense of self-worth is contingent on anything outside ourselves, it is guaranteed that we will compromise our values and end up in a world of inner conflict and/or numbness. For example, when faced with the choice between being honest and being liked, we will choose being liked and accepted, but we will have to tell ourselves we are honest in order to maintain a degree of emotional comfort. Ironically, to keep liking ourselves we will lie to ourselves, which is a self-defeating habit.

Living and leading from wholesome values truly transforms us. Our fundamental source of wellbeing has shifted from the fluid and unpredictable external world to an inner compass of goodness. The journey challenges us to the very core, but we set out courageously in order to gain the wisdom and peace that can only come from living in alignment with our most fundamental, life-serving values.

Why we're cynical about values

In my experience, most organisations (and their leaders) follow their stated values only to the degree that doing so does not cause any financial or reputational hardship. In other words, if following a wholesome value in any way threatens results or personal and company reputation, it will not be followed. Is it any wonder that we're so cynical about organisational values statements and branding efforts? Is it a surprise that people roll their eyes when we speak of them? They're just waiting for the values to be violated when they conflict with lower-level needs.

A social science study by researchers J. M. Darley and C. D. Batson drives home this point. The subjects were students at Princeton Theological Seminary—men who were studying to go into religious ministry. As each subject arrived, he was told he was to give a talk that would be recorded in another building. On the way to the venue, the subject encountered a 'victim' slumped in a doorway. The researchers wanted to know under what conditions the subject would stop to help.

Half of the subjects were assigned to talk on the parable of the Good Samaritan; the others were assigned a different topic. Some of the subjects were told they were late and should hurry; some were told they had just enough time to get to the recording room; and some were told they would arrive early.

The researchers found that 63 per cent of subjects who were in no hurry, 45 per cent of those in a moderate hurry and 10 per cent of those in a great hurry stopped to offer help. It made no difference whether the students were assigned to talk on the Good Samaritan parable, nor did it matter what their religious outlook was.

The point is this: When we are under pressure, we will invariably and routinely violate values we profess to hold dearly. Furthermore, we are most prone to lose our mindfulness when we are under pressure. Mindfulness is an essential partner to living our values in real time, when it counts.

When we 'put on sandals', with our values and mindfulness combined, we find the courage to be honest in difficult circumstances, to stay true to what we value when the pressure is on. We learn a precious secret: living with integrity is a beautiful practice in that it produces a more grounded, consistent experience of fulfilment.

Everyone wants to be led by leaders who consistently operate from wholesome values. The research supports this. We are inspired to engage more when our leaders walk their talk even—especially—when the pressure is on. When they don't, we become disillusioned and disengaged.

Two methods for staying on track with values

If we could be 100 per cent mindful all the time, we'd have the self-honesty required to notice when we've strayed from our values and the awareness to realign accordingly. But since we're not, we need methods for raising our self-awareness and keeping us on track. The two most effective methods for doing this are being in tune with our senses and being mindfully open to feedback.

Tuning in to our senses

In the introduction we discussed how self-awareness comes from tuning in to our body and senses. This has been demonstrated in my life time and time again.

One time I was shopping at the clothing store David Jones and found a good quality shirt on sale for 60 per cent off. I loved the shirt so I bought it. I took it home and put it on without undoing all the buttons. When I slipped it over my head, it ripped where it was still buttoned. I immediately had the thought, 'I know David Jones has a return policy, and I've still got my receipt. I'll tell them I was putting it on normally and it just ripped.'

It didn't take long before I felt a sick feeling in my stomach. Ordinarily, I probably would have tried to numb that feeling by getting something to eat and watching TV. But the nausea I felt was a barometer, a sort of warning signal telling me something was wrong. As I explored it mindfully, I was shocked and humbled to realise that my thoughtless decision essentially put the price tag for my integrity at the sale price of a shirt.

It made me wonder about boardroom discussions. If my integrity price tag is the value of a shirt, what's the price tag for leaders in business deals? I honestly felt a sense of despair. 'What chance have we really got for integrity when there's so much pressure around us to violate it?' I know from personal experience how tough it can be.

Thankfully, I was able to catch myself that day, primarily because I tuned in to what my body and senses were telling me. I took the shirt back and told them exactly what had happened, and much to my surprise they gave me a replacement. Contrary to what the ego would have us believe, following our integrity does not automatically mean financial loss.

Being open to feedback

Ideally, we would catch our own values violations by being self-aware as they occur. But because of our capacity for delusion, sometimes it takes feedback from others to realise when we've strayed from our values.

The first step to this, obviously, is to create a culture where feedback is welcome in the first place. Second is learning to accept feedback with grace and humility rather than reactivity. Both depend on our degree of mindfulness.

David Cooke, the managing director of the Japanese technology firm Konica Minolta in Australia, explained to me how his mindfulness practice over more than four decades has influenced his ability to accept criticism. 'I actually really enjoy when a challenging situation occurs, especially overt, full-frontal, head-butting criticism, because I think it's a great test. It's not like I'm some saint, but mindfulness helps you develop equanimity. With that equanimity, you have access to a solid anchor in yourself and you don't get overwhelmed so easily. So I find it quite fun when, in that relatively calm ocean, suddenly a big wave rises up. It makes life colourful and interesting.

'An example in my own life stands out. A year after my appointment as managing director I had reversed a mild decline in the company's financial results from the year before I took over. I produced the highest revenue figure, the highest profit figure, the highest number of unit sales and the best market share in the company's history. So I headed off to Japan for my first full-year review.

'As soon as I walked in, the man I report to in Tokyo, one of the global leaders in the company, said, "I'm so disappointed in you." And it was a great test, because here I was, with my ego, thinking I was going to get a pat on the back, and he said the exact opposite.

'I said to him very calmly, "May I ask what you're disappointed in?" And he said, "I just think you could have done so much better." He then proceeded to criticise and dismantle everything I had done.

'I love that the challenge came up and that my equanimity wasn't disturbed at all. Mindfulness practice has helped me to respond non-defensively to feedback. I want to understand that person's point of view, so I tend to ask questions. "Can you help me to understand why you're feeling like that?" The criticism may very well be valid, and that's gold. When somebody criticises you and there's some illumination around a personality trait or behaviour you weren't in touch with, that's an absolute blessing. I've learned to receive criticism without getting upset by it, to see it as a gift.'

How to skilfully establish organisational values

What are your organisational values? Can you list them immediately, or do you have to pause and think about it? If you're like most of the leaders I've worked with, it takes a while to remember your stated values. And if you can't remember them off the top of your head, what is the likelihood that they're actually influencing your behaviour in real time — especially when you're under pressure and duress? What's the likelihood that they've been deeply internalised?

This is not a judgement. When people have a hard time remembering their organisational values, it's not because they don't care about the values. Typically, it's because they haven't learned a skilful process for establishing and cultivating them.

With that understanding, here are the most important guidelines for establishing organisational values.

Less is more

It's fairly standard for organisations to establish five to ten core values and then execute a communication campaign around them. After the communication campaign they are forgotten and neglected, and business goes on as usual. Then, of course, people get cynical about them. The more values you list, the less likely people are to remember them. The less likely they are to remember them, the less likely they are to actually follow them in practice. Keep it simple. The fewer values you establish, the easier it is to remember and cultivate them.

Establish clear behavioural standards around your values

The entire purpose of establishing and cultivating values is to influence behaviour, which determines your culture. If your values don't influence behaviour, they are pointless.

Each value you establish should be accompanied with clear, tangible, observable and measurable behavioural standards. What does living this value look like in practice? How do we know when we've violated the value? How do we know when to correct course, and even what to fix? We can hold people accountable for values only by knowing the specific behaviours attached to those values.

When we state a value, we assume that we have a common understanding of it. But it's only in the description of the behaviour that we will know whether or not we mean the same thing by the value. If behaviours aren't clearly specified, we can't hold people accountable. We've got vagueness, and vagueness creates excuses on the part of those violating values, and shaming on the part of leaders trying to hold them accountable.

Create an agreed story around the values

There must be a shared story around each stated value and behavioural standard that helps leaders to bring it to life and into context. The story isn't written down; rather, it lives in the words and actions of the leadership and, by default, the organisation at large.

To give an example of these guidelines in action, one of my clients, an infrastructure company building one of the largest rail networks in the history of Australia, recently set their values with our support. Here is what they came up with:

Value: Integrity

Behavioural standards:

- We follow through on commitments.
- We say it as it is.

Value: Make a difference

Behavioural standards:

- We support each other to deliver our best.
- We always look to learn and improve.

Shared 'stories':

- **Follow through on commitments:** If we commit to a new behaviour, project deadline or anything else people inherently believe we have committed to, then we must take it extremely seriously and deliver—no excuses. If we know we won't be able to deliver, we need to have credible reasons and be proactive in communicating those reasons before any commitments are experienced as being broken.

- **Say it as it is:** We will not talk behind one another's back in this organisation, nor will we go home and complain about others at work if we have not had the discussion directly first. As leaders, we must make it safe for people to be honest; in fact, we must celebrate tough honesty so it is seen as a great thing to do in this organisation. We cannot leave meetings saying one thing and thinking something different. This will erode trust and ruin our culture. We need to say it as it is, and to consistently translate that into clear, observable facts and clear requests. We need to be constructive, not destructive in the way we say things, but above all we need to say it as it is.

- **Support each other to deliver our best:** We are fully committed to delivering the absolute best in everything we do. This means a true commitment to providing the tools, resources, coaching and empowerment to enable our people to shine. We recognise great achievements can't be made alone. We take the time to collaborate and to share information openly and freely. We seek to listen to and include others in order to draw on the best from everyone. We go out of our way to ensure our work has a positive impact on the greater community and the environment. We continually support each other in making safety a top-of-mind priority.

- **Always look to learn and improve:** We are always looking to challenge the status quo to find new and better ways of doing things. We embrace a culture of learning, which means we don't waste time looking to blame, defend and deny. Rather, we continually seek to learn from mistakes and integrate that learning. We commit to being curious and questioning, to taking a truly constructive approach to innovation and learning. We recognise the best way forward is often found through experimenting and taking risks—and that failure is inevitable when pushing into the unknown. We ensure there is a culture that makes it safe to fail. But we do so intelligently and never compromise safety. We never accept 'good enough'. We continually strive for excellence.

Breathe life into your values

Values are largely unconscious in organisations because too many of them are listed, they don't have clear behaviours attached to them, and leaders don't make them come alive and hold people accountable for them.

Once you've established your values, talk about them regularly. Demonstrate to people that you're serious about them. Recognise people who live them in their behaviour. Hold them up to show the organisation, 'This is what it looks like to live our values.' Hold people accountable for them uncompromisingly. The minute you compromise the values or allow others to, your team or organisation will become cynical about them.

One of my clients, Hilti Australia, does an amazing job of bringing their values to life, which is a primary reason why they won the Aon Hewitt Best of the Best Employer Award in 2011 and Best Employer every year since. I interviewed their learning and development manager, Anne Adamson, to find out how this remarkable organisation makes its values a daily part of the business. She explained that first of all they check for values in their recruitment phase by asking specific questions. They will ask potential recruits directly, for example, 'What are your personal values?' They are checking to see how well they align with their four core organisational values.

Once someone is hired, they are put through an induction process, the primary purpose of which is to instil the company values. They explain the desired culture and why it is important. They do exercises around the values. They provide a results/values matrix that shows it's not okay to get great results while violating their values, and vice versa. They take recruits through depth work on each of the values and explain exactly what they mean, how they are lived in daily work, and how they can be violated in terms of behaviour.

Ongoing values work includes periodic team camps, performance reviews (in which the values are included), reward systems based on living the values through peer nominations and the executive team revisiting the values regularly.

Jan Pacas, the general manager of Hilti Australia, also instituted the 'Champions League' recognition system to make the value of teamwork more tangible. He wanted to ensure that the people in support functions did not go unnoticed and were recognised as much as the sales force for top-level results. Jan created peer-nominated awards for people in non-managerial roles who had demonstrated outstanding customer focus. Anyone in the company could submit a nomination along with a story to support their nomination, which the Executive Management Team reviewed to make sure that the candidates consistently lived the company's values. Winners were determined over a nine-month period, and the awards were given out at a gala to celebrate Hilti's 50-year anniversary in Australia where 250 people gave the recipients a standing ovation for exemplifying the shared values.

I also discovered how alive the Hilti values are in their culture when I interviewed 13 people from the company after they had won the Best of the Best award. In each interview I casually slipped in the question, 'What are your organisational values?' With no warning or preparation time, 12 of the 13 could name all four instantly, and one of them remembered three out of four. I then asked them how they applied the values. All 13 explained clearly how the values applied to behavioural standards, performance reviews, informal recognition, hiring, decision-making and so on. *That* is making the values conscious and alive in the organisation.

The truth will set you free

We've discussed values and their relationship with leadership, mindfulness, wellbeing, trust and transformation. We've focused on honesty in particular because this value is so essential to credible leadership, healthy organisations and deeper levels of integrity.

But wait, there's more!

When I first discovered that I had deep self-worth wounds and I was endlessly trying to impress people, it was suggested to me that I practise 100 per cent vulnerable honesty as an antidote to my addiction to impressing, telling tall stories and the like. I remember thinking my teacher was insane. I was convinced that no one would find me worthy of connection if I was *totally* authentic, warts and all. But I took it on. I had seen the pain of my unworthiness all too clearly by that stage and I was ready to take a risk.

For eight straight years there was not a day that I did not wish for the practice to be easier. But in the end I discovered that vulnerable honesty is deeply, deeply healing. It taught me self-acceptance, that being broken is okay, being real is okay. In fact, my experience of connection with others became more profound as it was based on the truth, not a fake image.

There is so much more to honesty than telling the truth: there is a depth of self-awareness and realness that is profoundly rewarding. Honesty is what we want from leaders above all else. It's also something we all long for ourselves. This is the deepest definition for an 'authentic', no-bullshit leader. A leader we can trust not because they are perfect, but because they are authentic. They are not defending their flaws or hiding from you or themselves in their shadow. They can hear you, be real, be connected. And in doing so, they give you full permission to be human too. This is the heart of the deep, alive connection we all long for.

Find your compass and refer to it often

The mindful leader is grounded in and guided by wholesome, life-serving values. Mindfulness and values are mutually supportive. Mindfulness cultivates a values-based life, and values point us toward deeper mindfulness. It is a virtuous circle.

Leading from values is about so much more than boosting the bottom line. It's about creating a culture of wholeness and wellness. It's about bringing out the best in ourselves and others. It's about being true to ourselves. Ultimately, it's about creating peace in our hearts.

Mindfulness is so much more than just focus, concentration and freedom from stress. Without the context of wholesome, life-serving values, mindfulness is incomplete and does not achieve its ultimate 'why': the alleviation of suffering for all living beings. The Buddha spoke of the relationship between wisdom and ethics and compared them to two hands washing each other. You can't wash just one hand. Wisdom and ethics are mutually supportive.

Wholesome values, then, serve as a way to help us orient our mindfulness development into something deeply beneficial for ourselves and the world. They provide a guideline to remember what our behaviour looks like when we are inspiring and operating from a core of love, not fear.

Chapter 4

Inspire a mindful vision

I want it said of me by those who knew me best, that I always plucked a thistle and planted a flower where I thought a flower would grow.

Abraham Lincoln

Inspiring people with a shared vision is a primary task and critical test of leadership. Inspiring leaders envision the future by imagining exciting and even ennobling possibilities, and enlist others in a common vision by appealing to shared aspirations. Research by Jim Kouzes and Barry Posner shows that, next to honesty, being 'forward-looking'—in other words, visionary—is the second most admired characteristic people look for in leaders. The least effective leaders used this leadership practice 31 per cent less often than those seen as moderately effective leaders. The most effective leaders 'inspire a shared vision' about 54 per cent more often than those evaluated by their people as least effective. The least engaged people report that their leaders inspire a shared vision about 41 per cent less frequently than the leaders of the most engaged people.

As Jim and Barry explain, '[The] findings suggest that there's more to work than making money. People have a deep desire to make a difference. They want to know that they have done something on this earth, that there's a purpose to their existence … The best organizational leaders address this human longing by communicating the significance of the organization's work so that people understand their own unique role in creating and performing that work. When leaders clearly communicate a shared vision of an organization, they ennoble those who work on its behalf. They elevate the human spirit.'

Remember, the *why* of mindfulness is to reduce suffering and increase connection, wellbeing, joy and love for ourselves and for those whose lives we touch. It's far more than just about making us more focused, calm and productive; in fact, that is not and never has been the why for the practice itself. If you ask anyone why they want to be more productive, they will arrive back at the original why for mindfulness: to be happier, more engaged, more connected. This is the real point.

Mindful leaders leverage this deeper why by tapping into and awakening our innermost yearnings for meaning and purpose. They create a mindful vision for their teams and organisations — a vision focused on making a positive difference and alleviating suffering in the world, doing something that is good for everyone, not just for shareholders at the expense of other people or the planet. A mindful vision makes people whole again and awakens the best in them. When we know our organisation is making a positive difference, it opens our hearts to be present with the purpose of the business.

When considering what a mindful vision for a leader or organisation looks like, the criteria are simple: Does the vision and underlying intent of our organisation support connection, wellbeing, joy and love for ourselves and all our stakeholders? Does our core purpose support mindfulness, as defined by a deep sense of heartfelt engagement and presence, or does it stand in the way of engagement, thus leading to alienation, disconnection and suffering?

The statistics on global workplace engagement indicate we have a lot of work to do in this area. According to a 142-country study by Gallup, only 13 per cent of employees worldwide are engaged at work, engaged employees being defined as 'those who are involved in, enthusiastic about, and committed to their work and workplace'.

In other words, only about one in eight workers are psychologically committed to their job. Sixty-three per cent of workers are classified as 'not engaged', meaning they lack motivation and are less likely to invest discretionary effort in organisational goals or outcomes, while 24 per cent are 'actively disengaged', meaning they are unhappy and unproductive at work and likely to spread negativity in the workplace.[1]

The statistics suggest that in general our workplaces, and by implication the leaders of those workplaces, seem to be producing suffering and disengagement, the very opposite of the intent of mindfulness. It seems that most people are in a kind of psychological purgatory at work. Throwing a few mindfulness courses at people in these kinds of workplaces is like giving people stranded in a desert a bottle of water: it might help a little in the short term, but it doesn't provide a sustainable solution. Mindfulness is a challenging practice, and if the environment (leaders, culture) work against an engaged, honest, caring kind of mindfulness practice, it becomes nearly impossible to sustain. Furthermore, those people who practise mindfulness skilfully will leave because the dissonance will be too great as they 'wake up' to what is really going on.

But what if it could be different? What would it look like if leaders and organisations built a spirit of mindfulness into the very fabric of organisational leadership, vision, strategy and culture, and by doing so radically changed levels of engagement, happiness, loyalty and connection? What if team members could bring their whole selves to work and feel incredible pride and joy in what they do and who they do it for? And if this is possible, how can it be achieved?

Understanding human motivation

The conventional wisdom that external reward (for example, money) is the best way to engage people has been turned on its head by the extensive research detailed in the paradigm-shattering book *Drive: The Surprising Truth About What Motivates Us* by bestselling author Daniel Pink. When it comes to complex tasks requiring cognitive thinking, Pink says, standard rewards and punishments do not work.

Money does not motivate. What does motivate and engage people, studies show, are three factors:

- *autonomy*—meaning our desire to be self-directed. Pink explains that management is good if compliance is the goal. But if you want wholehearted engagement, self-direction is better.

- *mastery*—meaning the urge to constantly improve any skill we develop or project we undertake

- *purpose*—meaning the determination to make a positive contribution. Pink explains that when the profit motive is unmoored from the purpose motive, as it so often is in the corporate world, bad things happen, both ethically and in terms of quality and performance. Flourishing companies are those that are animated by a bigger purpose than profits alone.

In other words, the secret to high performance and satisfaction is the deeply human need for freedom, growth and creativity, and to make our world a better place. It's simply not exciting, inspiring or meaningful for people to work hard merely to increase 'shareholder value'. Such a goal, promoted so often in the corporate world, does not inspire people to give their best.

Inspiring people with an authentic mindful vision is one of the most important things a leader can do to boost engagement. A mindful vision is about creating an organisation with which people can connect emotionally, and in doing so enrich their lives, making them more meaningful and worthwhile. Mindful vision awakens the best in us by reconnecting us with what is most important, making it so much easier to be engaged and present at work.

Mindful livelihood: the basis of mindful vision

In the previous chapter we discussed the importance of embracing wholesome values. In addition, an integrated mindfulness practice includes mindful livelihood, which means being conscious in how we earn our living. Mindless or unconscious livelihood is easily identified as anything that involves lying, cheating, stealing, or doing harm to others or the environment. A mindless livelihood creates suffering for ourselves and others. Mindful livelihood is more than the absence of these destructive practices; it is the active and conscious pursuit of a better life for ourselves *and* others, and by extension the planet and communities that support our wellbeing.

Thich Nhat Hanh says, '[Y]ou have to find a way to earn your living without transgressing your ideals of love and compassion. The way you support yourself can be an expression of your deepest self, or it can be a source of suffering for you and others ... Our vocation can nourish our understanding and compassion, or erode them. We should be awake to the consequences, far and near, of the way we earn our living.' Mindfulness teacher S. N. Goenka adds, 'If the intention is to play a useful role in society in order to support oneself and to help others, then the work one does is [mindful] livelihood.'

Following the principle of mindful livelihood is how we find meaning in our work rather than just earning a salary. It is what we do to alleviate suffering through our work. When we connect our livelihood to making a positive difference for others, we are much more engaged and happy in our work. We make ourselves happier by making others happier. We transcend selfishness, rather than remaining mired in the pursuit of endless consumption.

There's nothing wrong with doing well for ourselves; in fact, the ethics of mindfulness naturally create the conditions for an abundant and joyful life. We cause suffering when we do well for ourselves at the expense of others. The only way we can psychologically sustain this is by turning away from the pain we cause others. As we turn away, we lose connection with life and ourselves. We numb our minds and bury the guilt under layers of distraction and busyness. It is simply not possible to stay connected, present and open-hearted and continue to cause others harm.

It doesn't make any sense to meditate regularly while working for a company that causes suffering for communities, the environment, suppliers or customers. In fact, the quality of meditation practice for someone in this position will likely always be poor because of the deep dissonance between their longing for inner peace and the nature of the organisation they support with their efforts. Mindful livelihood is the integration of our personal mindful practice with how we lead and operate our organisations. It is a truly holistic approach to awareness.

Another way of thinking about mindfulness is as *care-fulness*. Mindful livelihood means being full of care for the people within our organisation, the customers we serve and everyone on the planet, as well as the planet itself. It is caring about more than money and profit and personal gain; it is about being conscious of and sincerely caring about the impact we have on the world.

A vital source of wisdom for a mindful vision can be found in indigenous perspectives. For example, the Great Law of the Iroquois offers this inspirational guidance: 'In every deliberation, we must consider the impact on the seventh generation.' Dr Chellie Spiller (ChellieSpiller.com) has written extensively about applying indigenous insight in business. Reflecting on her Maori background, she explains, 'Care is at the heart of the Maori values system, which calls for humans to be kaitiaki, caretakers of the mauri, the life-force, in each other and in nature.'

This is a particular challenge for organisational leadership, given that, institutionally and legally, the first priority for businesses is financial. One company I know went through the process of becoming a publicly traded company. The executives who built the company had always cared deeply about making a positive difference, even at a cost to short-term profit. However, once they were listed, and finding themselves swept up in the all-consuming pursuit of maximising shareholder profit, they began to compromise on some of their longest held values. They were not necessarily 'wrong' either. They were simply fulfilling their legal duties to shareholders.

During a mindful leadership training session with them, the truth of what had been happening finally surfaced and was discussed with real honesty. They all admitted that something in their hearts had died. I felt incredibly sad to see them so disheartened. It certainly motivated me to keep writing this book. We really need a change. The Gallup stats show it, and my personal experience keeps confirming it.

Please remember that this is not just some nice, ethical, 'good guy' theory. Mindful livelihood—finding deeper meaning in work beyond mere financial rewards—is precisely what people want and need.

It pays to be conscious in business

All this Pollyanna-sounding talk of making a difference may have you thinking, 'That sounds great, but what about the bottom line? We have to make a profit to stay in business.' As it turns out, doing business consciously and mindfully actually boosts profits.

In their ground-breaking book *Firms of Endearment: How World-Class Companies Profit from Passion and Purpose*, Raj Sisodia, David Wolfe and Jag Sheth argue that a historic social transformation of capitalism is underway. 'Firms of Endearment (FoEs) are companies that have broadened their purpose beyond creating shareholder wealth to act as change agents for the larger good. They strive to align the interests of all stakeholders—customers, employees, partners, communities and shareholders—in such a way that no group gains at the expense of others. They are driven by a moral code and champion a new, humanistic vision of capitalism's role in society. They seek to maximise their value to society as a whole, not just to their shareholders. They seek to create emotional, experiential, social and financial value.'

The FoEs studied and highlighted by the authors demonstrate that doing good is great business. The publicly held FoEs returned 1026 per cent for investors over the 10 years ending 30 June 2006, compared with 122 per cent for the S&P 500; that's more than an eight to one ratio. Over a period of 15 years, FoEs have outperformed the S&P 500 by 14 times and Good to Great companies by six times.

In a Harvard University study, researchers analysed a wide range of investments across multiple industries to identify whether firms who focused on sustainability outperformed firms with no such focus. Sustainability in the study was defined as 'a firm's voluntary actions to manage its environmental and social impact and increase its positive contribution to society'. The overwhelming evidence was that 'firms with good ratings on material sustainability issues significantly outperform firms with poor ratings on these issues'.[2]

After finding a dramatic increase in the number of investors seeking to invest in sustainable companies, Goldman Sachs reported that 'more capital is now focused on sustainable business models, and the market is rewarding leaders and new entrants in a way that could scarcely have been predicted even fifteen years ago'.[3] The International Finance Corporation found that the Dow Jones Sustainability Index performed an average of 36.1 per cent better than the traditional Dow Jones Index over a period of five years. A Harvard Business School study concluded that 'high sustainability companies significantly outperform their counterparts over the long term, both in terms of stock market as well as accounting performance'.[4]

In other words, making a difference isn't just pie-in-the-sky idealism that makes the heart feel good; it's good business sense that the head can embrace as well.

Increased employee engagement is one explanation for this stellar performance. As the authors explain, people are looking for more than a salary from their work. They want work that engages their whole selves—not just their minds, but their hearts too. People want work that fulfils social needs and is therefore meaningful and psychologically rewarding. They want to see their work as a calling. In a study of 11 leading US and European business schools, 97 per cent of MBA graduates said they were willing to forgo financial benefits (14 per cent of expected income on average) to work with an organisation with a better reputation for corporate social responsibility and ethics.[5]

'Heart' messages around empathy, nurturing, caring and giving are not something we're used to hearing in business, but people are catching on that there is profit in bringing love into business. We've been trained to think primarily in terms of numbers and the bottom line. Talk of 'love' and other intangible qualitative dimensions often makes us uncomfortable. But it is attention to these dimensions that gives FoEs their competitive advantage.

A mindful vision is interdependent

Mindfulness teachers through the ages have taught that much of our suffering arises out of a feeling of separation. We feel alone and disconnected from other people and from the world. Within this state of isolation, we may create an island of connection with family members, friends, co-workers, organisations or sports teams to which we're attached. At times we build fences around our islands to protect and defend them. We might feel care and concern only for those on our tightly defined island and feel nothing for those outside it.

I grew up in South Africa during the last years of the apartheid era and became lost in what was a radical form of organised separation. I remember why Nelson Mandela was such an inspiration to me and why he has become a global hero. He refused to buy into the game of separation, and in doing so reminded us all that connection and interdependence are what our hearts long for most. He was a living example of what it means to lead courageously with a mindful intent, and he raised us all up with him.

In the pain of separation, we tend to shut down and it becomes a game of scarcity and pain. Corporations dump pollution into the environment. We attempt to dominate the earth and extract her resources with little or no thought of the future. Investment advisers swindle investors out of millions of dollars. We engage in class and race warfare. Every abuse of power and all the conflict we see in the world can be traced to the delusion of separation.

> *Through mindfulness we practise tuning in, reconnecting, engaging and being intimate with reality as it really is. And as we do we realise the self-evident truth of interdependence. In truth, there is no separation. Every word we speak and action we take has a tangible impact on us and on everyone else. Our level of consciousness — or lack thereof — makes a difference in the world.*

A mindful vision acknowledges and embraces this interdependence. Mindful leaders recognise that we are all in this together. They seek to create a vision of business that is conscious of its impact on all people and on the environment.

Albert Einstein said:

> ... Our task must be to ... [widen] our circle of compassion to embrace all living creatures and the whole of nature in its beauty ... We shall require a substantially new manner of thinking if humankind is to survive.

Mindfulness offers this 'substantially new manner of thinking' that can save us from the consequences of the delusion of separation.

From personal vision to shared vision

To be authentic, inspirational and influential, a mindful leader needs to have a personal vision for themselves and their own life before they can create a shared vision for a team or organisation. Developing personal vision is a process of deep discovery into the question, 'What is life about for me?' This question is critical because it sets the framework for our awareness and contains our energy. It pulls us out of fear, greed and delusion by defining our purpose beyond the endless race for comfort and flight from discomfort. It helps us know what is worth suffering for, what is worth sacrificing for. And this makes all the difference.

For a vision to be truly powerful, however, it must move from personal vision to shared vision. The leader's team and/or organisation must be aligned and engaged with the vision. The vision must live and breathe in the hearts of all team members. A leader must learn to translate what they see into something everyone can see, engage with and get excited about. An organisational vision is a shared vision. In other words, a leader cannot impose what's important to them exclusively. They must tap into meaning that everyone is excited about.

The good news is that when a vision is mindful, it springs from universal ideals that everyone yearns for and can get on board with. A mindful vision leaves the world a kinder, more wholesome, safer, better place. It treats suppliers, team members, the community and clients with love and does not objectify them as pawns. In short, it gives people exactly what they've always wanted from their workplace but rarely felt safe enough to assert.

I had an eye-opening experience with a client that drove this point home for me. They were working on repurposing their vision because their existing vision statements (about 'maximising shareholder returns' and the like) were the typical dry, impersonal stuff that people don't connect with or get inspired by. The leader asked everyone why they came to work. Everyone gave predictable and vague answers with very little meaning or inspiration in them. Then he asked them, 'Would you want your children to work here?' Almost everyone said no. He was astonished, and saddened.

In a team meeting the question on the table was, 'What is the purpose of our organisation?' Everyone was giving the same old dry, politically correct answers. This went on for a while until the leader slammed his hand on the table so hard it made his glasses fall off. He basically said, 'Let's cut the crap. I want to hear what is true for *you*, not what you think we should be saying to make everyone happy.'

With this intervention he broke through the ice of numbness, fear and conditioning, and everyone opened up and started answering with greater authenticity. The general theme was, 'We want to work for a company that betters people's lives and makes people happier.' The leader told me later, 'It was so refreshing because finally people were saying what was true in their hearts.'

We all have a deep yearning to contribute and make a positive difference. If we're not doing this, there is something missing in our lives. If a purpose or vision doesn't involve making the world a better place, it cannot nourish us. Like Abraham Lincoln, we too want to pluck thistles and plant flowers. It is in our DNA to want to make a difference and create a legacy, and 'maximising shareholder wealth' does nothing to tap into that yearning. A mindful vision is so engaging for us as human beings because it recovers meaning in business.

Putting your money where your mouth is

Business is often demonised for practices that harm the planet and bring out the worst in people. In all honesty, some of this criticism is merited. The new trend for socially conscious business, however, embraces the good in business while transforming the harmful aspects. It recognises that business can be a profound force for good — if leaders have the right intention.

The shift in business to a more humanistic approach, to serving a more wholesome purpose beyond simply making money, has been building for quite some time. It has many manifestations, including the conscious capitalism movement, Richard Branson's B Team movement, social entrepreneurship, green building (such as LEED certifications), microfinance, organic food production, fair trade standards and impact investing.

At the heart of the movement is a new corporate entity certification process that formalises the ideals of conscious capitalism: B Corporations, the 'B' standing for benefit. B Corps are privately assessed, audited and certified by the non-profit B Lab (BCorporation. net) to meet rigorous standards addressing the following factors:

- *governance*— the company's transparency and the extent to which social and environmental considerations are ingrained in the management and legal responsibilities

- *workers*—the company's contribution to the financial, social, physical and professional wellbeing of its employees, including compensation and benefits, work environment and ownership opportunities

- *community*—the company's contribution to the economic and social wellbeing of the communities in which it operates, including job creation and inclusivity, civic engagement and philanthropy, and suppliers

st emotionally intelligent and successful team players

rdt, CEO of Pharos Systems (Pharos.com)

k of mindfulness as being present—being truly awake what is before us and growing our openness to explore With this understanding, finding the link between and B Corps seems straightforward. By growing the t of our business to serve in the world in a conscious, way we are executing 'corporate mindfulness'. Our ntra calls us to be present to the impact our products world and acts as a siren call of awareness to our business

, CEO of Brand Cool (BrandCool.com)

s question through several lenses because of the different y that impact how I engage in the world.

dfulness practitioner and teacher I see being a certified s a form of skilful means. There is an inner and an outer he inner aspect involves intention, the intention to be of the world. The outer aspect is action, the way we operate nesses and the kind of work we do. Being a B Corp is love passion in action through business.

lue of the actual certification is much like the value of taking r holding a precept. As a CEO I appreciate this because it's a tment that keeps my business operating within the boundary ntention, an intention that is shared by my employees and the g B Corp community.

ly, I would say that the B Corp movement is a sane response r current circumstances. It's fundamentally about relationship. can business be in a sane relationship with its employees, mers and suppliers, its communities, the environment and the omic framework in which we find ourselves?

B Corp movement is rooted in a deep understanding of rdependence. It's a force for positive change as it calls on us to g greater consciousness and care to all our business relationships, aping and amplifying the best of capitalism, while gently rming the aspects that no longer serve.'

- *environment*—the company's efforts to reduce its environmental footprint, as created by company facilities, input materials, outputs/wastes and suppliers/distributors

- *impact business model*—beyond the operations of the business, whether the company is designed to create a positive social and/or environmental impact, including product impact and providing those in need with basic services.

At the time of writing, more than 20 000 businesses are actively measuring their performance through the B Corps' B Impact Assessment, and more than 1500 organisations in more than 42 countries have gained enough points to be formally certified. These include a wide range of businesses across more than 130 industries, from famous US companies like Ben & Jerry's, Etsy and Patagonia to Triodos Bank, a well-known European bank; Plum Organics, a baby food brand; Greyston Bakery, which creates job opportunities for ex-cons and homeless people; Natura, a large public company in Brazil providing personal care products; Roshan, a telecommunications company and one of the largest employers in Afghanistan; and five:am, a producer of cereals and yoghurts in Australia.

Compared with other sustainable businesses, B Corps are:

- 68 per cent more likely to donate at least 10 per cent of profits to charity

- 55 per cent more likely to cover at least some health insurance costs for employees

- 47 per cent more likely to use on-site renewable energy

- 45 per cent more likely to give bonuses to non-executive members

- 28 per cent more likely to include women and minorities in management

- 18 per cent more likely to use suppliers from low-income communities.

I was privileged to meet and interview Jay Coen Gilbert, one of the founders of B Lab and a personal hero of mine. He explained that most people come to B Lab wondering, 'Why should I act differently in business?' Once they understand the answers to that question, their next questions become, '*How* can I formalise this intention to make a difference? What does it actually mean to be a conscious capitalist? What formal steps should I take or what practical changes should I implement? How do I create more positive impact with my business or with my money?'

B Lab gives them a roadmap and a tool kit. The road map is their B Impact Assessment, which, Jay says, 'is not to tell you what to do, but to show you all the opportunities and choices you have'. B Lap then helps you benchmark how you're doing along your journey, compared with your past performance or your future goals, or compared with others on the same path. This is important, Jay explains, because it 'brings in a behavioural psychology element that is powerful for motivating behaviour change, which is, "How are other people like me doing, and how am I comparing?" Comparison is deeply rooted in our psyche, so giving people that kind of comparative data in a fun, positive, affirming way, along with tools to take the next step, is where we see our role.'

One thing that struck me about the B Corp model is that the certification applies only to for-profit businesses. Again, the point is that, contrary to what many people think, business can be a force for good. With business representing three-quarters of economic activity and the greater part of our lives spent engaging in the marketplace, Jay and his partners felt that the greatest opportunity for making an impact was in harnessing the power of business, but for a higher purpose than just making money.

When I asked Jay how he saw the mindfulness movement in the context of B Corps his answer was simple but profound: 'B Corps are mindfulness in the marketplace. Nothing more, nothing less. And on a more personal note, we want to make our parents proud and we want our children to be proud of us. We want to leave this world knowing we made a difference. B Corps gives us a path and

a toolkit for doing this. T. mindful business.'

Phil Vernon, a mindful. Ethical, a certified B Corp funds based on strict criteri illustrates how attractive the From a long career in financia how misaligned his personal v the corporate world engaged i that would incorporate and eml not have to put on a 'work mask

He told me, 'Global corporati some nation states, have the dom our planet and everything that li the corporation intrinsically doesn is intrinsically profit and self-intere. change. We need a new business m compassion in the way the business B Corp concept is all about.'

I asked several other B Corp CEC saw their B Corp certification and t linked. These were their responses.

Spencer Sherman, Founder and . Abacus Wealth Partners (AbacusWe. *The Cure for Money Madness*

'For me, mindfulness combines an intentio with an attention to our inner sensations a is acting from the wisdom of our hearts, r thoughts or fears. Becoming a B Corp me extension of that. Doing good in the world h a more profitable business. I'm here to share and make a positive impact. B Corps are all doing good. The two are correlated for me. \ others, I'm happier and much more likely to wi

Conscious business isn't easy

At this point I must make an admission: As mindful as I try to be, I struggle with conscious capitalism as much as anyone. It's not an easy process. It requires a commitment that can directly challenge our fear, greed and attachment. This was made clear to me when I realised I could certify my own company as a B Corp and started going through the process. I learned the requirements, which include giving a percentage of turnover or profit to charity, donating pro bono time, extensive documentation, and using responsible banking practices and suppliers, among others.

Halfway through the process, which was taking me quite a bit of time and effort, I started feeling like I wanted to back out of it. To put it frankly, I got scared when I started thinking of the short-term financial implications. I started wondering, for example, whether as the sole income earner for my family I could afford to give more money to charity. A strong resistance arose in me. At one point I was sitting in front of my computer with the assessment and my internal dialogue was, 'I know this is a good thing, but maybe I'm not ready for it yet. Maybe I should wait until next year.' I felt a familiar tuning out, a sudden longing to look at Facebook or YouTube, to turn away.

But this time I turned inward instead. I closed my eyes, took some deep breaths and got really quiet inside myself. At that moment, I gave my heart a voice, which said, 'Michael, there is no choice but to continue because any other choice will break your heart. You need to do this for yourself. You have an opportunity to take another step toward alleviating suffering in yourself and in those you serve, and you know that is what is most important to you. You've felt the pain in the corporate world, and now you understand that much of it derives from the very structure of business. This will give your business an even higher meaning and allow you to model the way and be congruent in an even deeper way.' I am proud to report that my business is now a certified B Corp.

It was fascinating to me to feel that inner resistance to becoming a more conscious business, even when that is what I hold most dear. It was a lesson to me on how if we don't stay mindful, we can sabotage our highest ideals through fear, numbing and clinging.

How anyone at any level can make a difference

It's great when owners and top executives make the decision to lead a more mindful business. But what can we do to make a difference when we don't have complete control over how our team or organisation operates? What can a mid-level manager, or anyone at any level, do to impact the consciousness of an organisation?

First of all, understand that you have complete control over your personal purchasing and investment decisions. You can be a force for good simply through how you run your household, even if you have little or no control over how your company operates.

Second, understand that leadership is a mindset, not a title. As Jay Coen Gilbert explained, there are many examples of new conscious business practices adopted by organisations that were initiated by single individuals at all levels. These are leadership-minded people who raised their hands and said, 'Couldn't we do this better? What if we were to change this?' Jay recommends that people choose just *one* thing that they care about and may be able to implement on their own, or that they are passionate enough about to gather support for the idea. Executives will change something if a lot of employees are on board with an idea and push for change.

The next obvious question is, what exactly should you do to make your company more conscious? When I asked Jay this, thinking that B Lab would have some sort of checklist, his answer was, 'I'd rather not be prescriptive about what people should do, because the ideal scenario is people initiating mindful action themselves. So I would tell people to find something that they care about personally, and work to make that happen. If you need some basic orientation, though, a great place to start would be to look at our B Impact Assessment

- *environment*—the company's efforts to reduce its environmental footprint, as created by company facilities, input materials, outputs/wastes and suppliers/distributors
- *impact business model*—beyond the operations of the business, whether the company is designed to create a positive social and/or environmental impact, including product impact and providing those in need with basic services.

At the time of writing, more than 20 000 businesses are actively measuring their performance through the B Corps' B Impact Assessment, and more than 1500 organisations in more than 42 countries have gained enough points to be formally certified. These include a wide range of businesses across more than 130 industries, from famous US companies like Ben & Jerry's, Etsy and Patagonia to Triodos Bank, a well-known European bank; Plum Organics, a baby food brand; Greyston Bakery, which creates job opportunities for ex-cons and homeless people; Natura, a large public company in Brazil providing personal care products; Roshan, a telecommunications company and one of the largest employers in Afghanistan; and five:am, a producer of cereals and yoghurts in Australia.

Compared with other sustainable businesses, B Corps are:

- 68 per cent more likely to donate at least 10 per cent of profits to charity
- 55 per cent more likely to cover at least some health insurance costs for employees
- 47 per cent more likely to use on-site renewable energy
- 45 per cent more likely to give bonuses to non-executive members
- 28 per cent more likely to include women and minorities in management
- 18 per cent more likely to use suppliers from low-income communities.

I was privileged to meet and interview Jay Coen Gilbert, one of the founders of B Lab and a personal hero of mine. He explained that most people come to B Lab wondering, 'Why should I act differently in business?' Once they understand the answers to that question, their next questions become, '*How* can I formalise this intention to make a difference? What does it actually mean to be a conscious capitalist? What formal steps should I take or what practical changes should I implement? How do I create more positive impact with my business or with my money?'

B Lab gives them a roadmap and a tool kit. The road map is their B Impact Assessment, which, Jay says, 'is not to tell you what to do, but to show you all the opportunities and choices you have'. B Lap then helps you benchmark how you're doing along your journey, compared with your past performance or your future goals, or compared with others on the same path. This is important, Jay explains, because it 'brings in a behavioural psychology element that is powerful for motivating behaviour change, which is, "How are other people like me doing, and how am I comparing?" Comparison is deeply rooted in our psyche, so giving people that kind of comparative data in a fun, positive, affirming way, along with tools to take the next step, is where we see our role.'

One thing that struck me about the B Corp model is that the certification applies only to for-profit businesses. Again, the point is that, contrary to what many people think, business can be a force for good. With business representing three-quarters of economic activity and the greater part of our lives spent engaging in the marketplace, Jay and his partners felt that the greatest opportunity for making an impact was in harnessing the power of business, but for a higher purpose than just making money.

When I asked Jay how he saw the mindfulness movement in the context of B Corps his answer was simple but profound: 'B Corps are mindfulness in the marketplace. Nothing more, nothing less. And on a more personal note, we want to make our parents proud and we want our children to be proud of us. We want to leave this world knowing we made a difference. B Corps gives us a path and a toolkit for doing this. They give us a formal structure for enabling mindful business.'

Phil Vernon, a mindfulness practitioner, the CEO of Australian Ethical, a certified B Corp investment firm that creates managed funds based on strict criteria of ethics and sustainability, perfectly illustrates how attractive the 'mindful business model' is becoming. From a long career in financial services, he came to the realisation of how misaligned his personal values were with some of the practices the corporate world engaged in. He actively sought out a company that would incorporate and embody his personal values so he would not have to put on a 'work mask', as he put it.

He told me, 'Global corporations, many of which are larger than some nation states, have the dominant influence over the future of our planet and everything that lives on it. That's an issue because the corporation intrinsically doesn't have any compassion because it is intrinsically profit and self-interest oriented. The system needs to change. We need a new business model that embeds empathy and compassion in the way the business conducts itself. That's what the B Corp concept is all about.'

I asked several other B Corp CEOs to share with me how they saw their B Corp certification and their mindfulness practice as linked. These were their responses.

Spencer Sherman, Founder and Executive Chairman of Abacus Wealth Partners (AbacusWealth.com) and author of *The Cure for Money Madness*

'For me, mindfulness combines an intention to do good in the world with an attention to our inner sensations and experience. The key is acting from the wisdom of our hearts, rather than our random thoughts or fears. Becoming a B Corp member was an effortless extension of that. Doing good in the world has brought me joy and a more profitable business. I'm here to share my gifts with others and make a positive impact. B Corps are all about doing well by doing good. The two are correlated for me. When I'm impacting others, I'm happier and much more likely to win more business and attract the most emotionally intelligent and successful team players to Abacus.'

Kevin Pickhardt, CEO of Pharos Systems (Pharos.com)

'I like to think of mindfulness as being present—being truly awake and aware of what is before us and growing our openness to explore this fully. With this understanding, finding the link between mindfulness and B Corps seems straightforward. By growing the commitment of our business to serve in the world in a conscious, harmonious way we are executing 'corporate mindfulness'. Our B Corp mantra calls us to be present to the impact our products have on the world and acts as a siren call of awareness to our business practices.'

Sue Kochan, CEO of Brand Cool (BrandCool.com)

'I view this question through several lenses because of the different roles I play that impact how I engage in the world.

'As a mindfulness practitioner and teacher I see being a certified B Corp as a form of skilful means. There is an inner and an outer aspect. The inner aspect involves intention, the intention to be of benefit in the world. The outer aspect is action, the way we operate our businesses and the kind of work we do. Being a B Corp is love and compassion in action through business.

'The value of the actual certification is much like the value of taking a vow or holding a precept. As a CEO I appreciate this because it's a commitment that keeps my business operating within the boundary of my intention, an intention that is shared by my employees and the growing B Corp community.

'Finally, I would say that the B Corp movement is a sane response to our current circumstances. It's fundamentally about relationship. How can business be in a sane relationship with its employees, customers and suppliers, its communities, the environment and the economic framework in which we find ourselves?

'The B Corp movement is rooted in a deep understanding of interdependence. It's a force for positive change as it calls on us to bring greater consciousness and care to all our business relationships, reshaping and amplifying the best of capitalism, while gently reforming the aspects that no longer serve.'

Conscious business isn't easy

At this point I must make an admission: As mindful as I try to be, I struggle with conscious capitalism as much as anyone. It's not an easy process. It requires a commitment that can directly challenge our fear, greed and attachment. This was made clear to me when I realised I could certify my own company as a B Corp and started going through the process. I learned the requirements, which include giving a percentage of turnover or profit to charity, donating pro bono time, extensive documentation, and using responsible banking practices and suppliers, among others.

Halfway through the process, which was taking me quite a bit of time and effort, I started feeling like I wanted to back out of it. To put it frankly, I got scared when I started thinking of the short-term financial implications. I started wondering, for example, whether as the sole income earner for my family I could afford to give more money to charity. A strong resistance arose in me. At one point I was sitting in front of my computer with the assessment and my internal dialogue was, 'I know this is a good thing, but maybe I'm not ready for it yet. Maybe I should wait until next year.' I felt a familiar tuning out, a sudden longing to look at Facebook or YouTube, to turn away.

But this time I turned inward instead. I closed my eyes, took some deep breaths and got really quiet inside myself. At that moment, I gave my heart a voice, which said, 'Michael, there is no choice but to continue because any other choice will break your heart. You need to do this for yourself. You have an opportunity to take another step toward alleviating suffering in yourself and in those you serve, and you know that is what is most important to you. You've felt the pain in the corporate world, and now you understand that much of it derives from the very structure of business. This will give your business an even higher meaning and allow you to model the way and be congruent in an even deeper way.' I am proud to report that my business is now a certified B Corp.

It was fascinating to me to feel that inner resistance to becoming a more conscious business, even when that is what I hold most dear. It was a lesson to me on how if we don't stay mindful, we can sabotage our highest ideals through fear, numbing and clinging.

How anyone at any level can make a difference

It's great when owners and top executives make the decision to lead a more mindful business. But what can we do to make a difference when we don't have complete control over how our team or organisation operates? What can a mid-level manager, or anyone at any level, do to impact the consciousness of an organisation?

First of all, understand that you have complete control over your personal purchasing and investment decisions. You can be a force for good simply through how you run your household, even if you have little or no control over how your company operates.

Second, understand that leadership is a mindset, not a title. As Jay Coen Gilbert explained, there are many examples of new conscious business practices adopted by organisations that were initiated by single individuals at all levels. These are leadership-minded people who raised their hands and said, 'Couldn't we do this better? What if we were to change this?' Jay recommends that people choose just *one* thing that they care about and may be able to implement on their own, or that they are passionate enough about to gather support for the idea. Executives will change something if a lot of employees are on board with an idea and push for change.

The next obvious question is, what exactly should you do to make your company more conscious? When I asked Jay this, thinking that B Lab would have some sort of checklist, his answer was, 'I'd rather not be prescriptive about what people should do, because the ideal scenario is people initiating mindful action themselves. So I would tell people to find something that they care about personally, and work to make that happen. If you need some basic orientation, though, a great place to start would be to look at our B Impact Assessment

(BImpactAssessment.net) to see all the different opportunities there are to make a difference with your business.'

Jay gave the example of the company Etsy, which took an entire day to have every employee brainstorm all the ways they could use the company as a greater force for good. They used the B Impact Assessment to consider opportunities. One person who read the question, 'What percentage of your employees are people with disabilities?' got excited about the possibilities. They started thinking of what jobs could be done by people with physical or mental disabilities. They identified a position, and the person who had the original idea found an agency that helps train and bring people with intellectual disabilities into the workforce. They found and hired a person, who ended up being perfect for the position.

It started with one person asking one simple question, which triggered some reflection and led to action. Anyone can look at the questions in the B Impact Assessment and go through a similar process. Find one issue that resonates with you and then do what you can to raise the question within your company and make an impact.

Ethical investing: extending our mindfulness from how we earn to how we spend

I have briefly mentioned conscious investing. Here I want to explore this further because it's another great opportunity for mindful leaders to make a difference.

To find out more I interviewed Rodger Spiller, an authorised financial adviser, certified financial planner, certified responsible investment adviser and founder of Money Matters, an investment firm that provides 'responsible investments for ethical investors' (MoneyMatters.co.nz). Rodger has also been a mindfulness practitioner for years and is a leadership development expert. When I asked him how he defined mindful investing, he replied, 'Mindful investors wisely realise that what they do with their money matters.

They care about the impact of their money and take action to invest responsibly, integrating environmental, social and governance issues into investment decision-making and ownership practices. Mindful investors are part of the solution rather than the problem. They encourage companies to address the world's environmental and social challenges as business opportunities. They know what their money is up to—what the companies in which they invest do and how well these companies relate to their stakeholders. They seek to make money *and* make a difference—to do well and do good.'

Along with the rise of conscious business, socially responsible investing has also experienced a surge in popularity in recent years. According to the Global Sustainable Investment Review, responsible investment assets grew by 61 per cent between 2012 and 2014, when they totalled US$21.4 trillion. This represented 30 per cent of professionally managed assets in the regions covered, up from 21.5 per cent two years earlier.[6]

What's driving the trend, researchers say, is rapidly growing client demand as well as the increasing understanding that environmental, social and governance issues are ever more critical drivers of investment value. Rosabeth Moss Kanter, of Harvard Business School, argued in 1991, 'Money should never be separated from mission. It is an instrument, not an end. Detached from values, it may indeed be the root of all evil. Linked effectively to social purpose, it can be the root of opportunity.'

Each of us can vote mindfully with our dollars, in terms of both how we spend and how we invest. As our mindfulness grows through sustained practice, we become increasingly sensitive to the impact we have on the world through all our activities, economic and otherwise.

Change happens one person at a time

In his magical book *The Unexpected Universe*, anthropologist, natural science writer and philosopher Loren Eiseley wrote of 'The Star Thrower'. It was a story that struck a chord with many readers and has since been adapted and retold countless times, and it wonderfully illustrates how mindful leaders can make a difference.

An old man is walking along the sea shore, which is littered with starfish after a big storm has passed and the tide begins to ebb. Off in the distance he sees a small figure on the otherwise deserted beach. Slowly they converge and he makes out a young boy, walking slowly and pausing often as he bends down to pick up an object and throw it out over the sea.

As the boy approaches, the man calls out, 'Good morning! May I ask what you are doing?'

The young boy replies, 'Throwing starfish into the ocean. The tide has washed them up too high for them to return to the sea by themselves, and when the sun gets higher they will die.'

'But there must be tens of thousands of them. I'm afraid you won't make much of a difference.'

The boy stoops, picks up another starfish and hurls it far out into the sea. Then he turns and smiles. 'It made a difference to that one!'

We can't do everything, but we can do something. And it starts with creating a mindful vision of how we can make a difference in the world, both personally and organisationally.

Chapter 5

Cultivate beginner's mind

The only true wisdom is in knowing you know nothing.

Socrates

To lead is to step into the unknown. Leaders cross boundaries and take us to places we have never been before. The art of discovery is the heart of great leadership. No organisation ever became a leader by following the best practices of others. We can learn from and build on the lessons and successes of others, but ultimately a leader must blaze a trail into unknown territory.

The best leaders are those who constantly push us to find new and better ways to do things, to explore and discover, to conquer limitations. They take initiative. They accept risk as an opportunity to learn and grow. They are constantly innovating, searching for new opportunities—'challenging the process', as Jim Kouzes and Barry Posner put it. This both allows their organisations to adapt to change and increases the engagement of their team members.

Research by Jim and Barry shows that people who feel challenged to innovate, learn and improve exhibit higher levels of engagement than those who are not challenged. People who are challenged by their leaders are significantly more likely to feel committed to the success of the organisation and proud to tell others that they work for the organisation. They also show greater motivation than those reporting only occasionally feeling challenged by their leaders. The same results hold true for the leaders themselves. The most effective leaders challenge the process 46 per cent more than leaders evaluated as least effective by their team members. Furthermore, the least engaged team members report that their leaders exhibit this leadership discipline about 36 per cent less often than the leaders of the most engaged people.

Change or decline

Change can be scary and risky. It directly confronts our deep desire for permanence, stability and security in an impermanent, uncertain world. But in today's world, resisting change is the riskiest thing we can do. The acronym VUCA (for volatility, uncertainty, complexity and ambiguity) has been used in recent years to describe technological, social and organisational conditions that seem to be changing at an almost exponential rate.

Architect, theorist and inventor Buckminster Fuller proposed that 5000 years ago an invention or innovation that changed what he called 'the critical path of humanity' came along about every 200 years. By AD 1 the interval had decreased to 50 years, and by AD 1000, 30 years. By the Renaissance, an invention that changed the nature of our world was emerging every three years; by the Industrial Revolution, it was happening every six months; and by the 1920s, Fuller estimated, the interval was down to 90 days. He called this extraordinary process 'accelerating acceleration'. Physicist Peter Russell suggests the interval between important new breakthroughs is now down to days, if not hours.

Organisations that are unable to keep up with or adapt to change will not survive. One client recently told me they don't even do strategic planning any more because the world is moving too fast for fixed strategies, which can often be obsolete before they have even been embedded. Their CEO said, 'The best we can do is to learn faster and see emergent opportunities faster than anyone else.' I wouldn't have expected to hear such a perspective even as recently as five years ago.

To maintain the status quo as an organisation in the modern world is to decline and die. Successful organisations are those that can continually flex, learn and adjust, and do so nimbly and quickly. The ability to learn quickly has become more important than capital, market share or almost any other factor. Creating a culture of perpetual innovation is far more important than any business strategy you could devise. And the culture is determined by the behaviour and mindset of the leaders.

This means leaders must be in touch with the ever-changing flow of life. They must learn to pay attention, to connect the dots and recognise patterns before others do. They must be equipped with the right tools for dealing not only with uncertainty itself, but also with their own mindset and fears in relation to uncertainty. The discipline of 'beginner's mind', as taught and cultivated by mindfulness, provides the key.

Beginner's mind

Beginner's mind is an aspect of mindfulness practice in action. It is about viewing the world and our experiences with an innocent mind devoid of preconceptions, expectations, judgements and prejudices. Attitudinally, it is beautifully summed up in these words by Socrates: 'I would rather be proved wrong than right.' It is to explore and observe things with a deep sense of openness, much as a child explores the world with curiosity and wonder and no fixed point of view. It is to lose our 'expert's mind', which tends to be rigid, fixed and calcified. When we view the world through expert's mind, we think we know all the answers and are therefore closed to new possibilities.

A famous Zen story illustrates this. A professor of Buddhism once visited a Japanese master. After listening to the professor's impressive level of intellectual knowledge of Zen, the master served tea. When his visitor's cup was full, the master kept pouring. Tea spilled out of the cup and over the table.

'The cup is full!' protested the professor. 'No more will go in!'

'Like this cup,' said the master, 'you are full of your own opinions and speculations. How can I show you Zen unless you first empty your cup?'

In expert's mind, we are terrified of 'I don't know'. But in beginner's mind, we recognise that 'I don't know' is powerful, for it is the beginning of wisdom. Whenever you admit that you don't know something, it's a good sign that new insights and understanding will follow. For many leaders, feeling we don't know is scary, because we're expected to have the answers. People look to us for guidance, so we often pretend to know more than we do because we think that having the answers is what gives us credibility. In fact, the opposite is true.

Most of the time, when we think we know, we don't really know at all. All we know are our past impressions of a situation that is happening now, the conclusions we came to on previous occasions, or judgements about similar events or circumstances that happened in the past. 'I know' can actually be a great handicap that keeps us entrenched in the past and out of the present. It allows for nothing new—no surprises, insights or discoveries. Fresh insights and wisdom remain elusive because we are locked into fixed judgements of the past.

As Kevin Pickhardt from Pharos put it, 'If we're going to view ourselves as either expert or beginner, I'd rather err on the side of beginner. As soon as we see ourselves as experts, learning begins to slow. I like to embrace learning—it keeps us young and sharp and helps us create the culture we want, which means not assuming we know the answers.'

Beginner's mind has various qualities to it. One quality is a soft, open receptivity, not of active inquiry but rather of a restful, gentle, easy openness. It's like enjoying a sunset restfully, with a fresh, open mind. It's an uncontracted state, free of the usual confinement of fixed beliefs, viewpoints and ideas.

Beginner's mind can also be far more intense, embracing a sense of keen inquiry and active curiosity. We are intensely focused and keenly curious about what is happening in and around us.

Beginner's mind is much more than a technique; it is an *attitude*. It's an attitude of curiosity that lives within you, a reflection of your desire to know the truth of things and the nature of reality as it presents itself. It also takes the courage to be willing to ask big questions that may shake the foundations of your life and confront you with issues you might rather avoid.

Beginner's mind is the art of questioning all of one's assumptions, beliefs and interpretations as a means of opening up space in the mind for a deeper wisdom to arise. Watch. Stay patient with the sometimes disorienting sense of the unknown. The critical moments of insight come when you least expect them—when your mind is truly open.

Taking time to allow that space to open up is vital. Libby Klingberg, owner of Explore & Develop North Ryde and Macquarie Park Childcare Centres, told me that for her the ability to slow down and give herself time to make decisions has been a primary benefit of mindfulness practice. As she put it, 'I now give myself more time to come up with the right answers and find the right direction to take my staff in. I used to think I needed fast and decisive action. Now I am more likely to say, "I am not sure right now. I would like to think about this and I will get back to you." And when people who expect immediate responses are not happy about this, I have found that I do not have the same emotional response when I have allowed myself more professional breathing room.'

The practice of beginner's mind is particularly relevant during times of change. James Sheffield, a general manager at Commonwealth Bank of Australia, is a phenomenal example of this. He shared with me that because of his mindfulness practice, he has learned to accept change much better.

'In large organisations there's always an ebb and flow and cycles of change, particularly changes in leadership. With each change you have to adapt to new thinking. There's a tendency to resist change and think, "This isn't as good as it was before." But thinking of it mindfully, it is what it is—it's not worse and it's not better, it's just different. When you accept the differences, good things appear that you might not have seen before. I've learned to stop looking at the negativity I see in changes and to focus on the positives. Otherwise, you get obsessed with looking over your shoulder at what was and you never live in the present. It's not a survival mechanism, it's just staying open and curious. It's different, so learn from it.'

James made it through one particularly difficult period, when he thought he was going to lose his job, by continually asking himself, 'What am I going to learn from this?' Every day when he came home he would ask, 'What have I learned today?' He would even give a prayer of gratitude: 'Thank you for giving me this chance to learn.' He said, 'Without mindfulness training my reaction would have been a meltdown. I would have said, "Stuff this," walked out and found another job. I would have run away. But you don't deal with your own development by running away.'

James continually develops himself by trying new things. He never learned how to swim because he was terrified of the water. So he set himself the goal of changing that and he now swims long distances regularly. He received his black belt in Tae Kwon Do after three and a half years of focusing. This is important, he says, because we tend to stay in positions where we can play to our strengths. We avoid anything that might expose weakness or incompetence, and that keeps us fearful and stagnant.

'I've learned to enjoy putting myself into situations where I don't know anything and feel like I'm a child and learning again. It's really invigorating. As adults we stop learning like children and we become closed. We start to circumscribe the box in which we live, and therefore we slowly start to die. You're not living your life if you're not pushing yourself to go out of your depth and competency and learn more. You've got to be open to new experiences and to perceptions other than your own.'

Cultivating beginner's mind is a cornerstone of seeing life as it is with fresh eyes and a mind open to new possibilities. With beginner's mind comes wisdom beyond knowledge, and a deeper sense of security and ease. In his book *The Art of Taking Action*, Gregg Krech wrote, 'I love hanging out with three year-olds. I love the way that they see the world, because they're seeing the world for the first time.

I love the way that they can stare at a bug crossing the sidewalk. I love the way that they'll stare slack-jawed at their first baseball game with wide eyes and a mitt on their hand, soaking in the crack of the bat and the crunch of the peanuts and the smell of the hotdogs. I love the way that they'll spend hours picking dandelions in the backyard and putting them into a nice centerpiece for Thanksgiving dinner. I love the way that they see the world, because they're seeing the world for the first time. Having a sense of awareness is just about embracing your inner three-year-old.'

When we cultivate beginner's mind we become one with the flow of life. We are not at odds with life as it actually is, but our minds tend to fixate in fear. We make solid that which is not solid. We fear the constant shift and change of things.

Fixed or expert's mind indicates a mind that is not relaxed and at ease. When we work with our minds and hearts, we develop a capacity to be flexible and open. But it takes being free from fixed mind and not getting caught in our strongly held views and opinions. It takes not reducing everything to labels, not reducing things down to something you can hold in your hand and hold onto and feel safe about. It takes relaxing the mind. In this state, what you can experience and learn is limitless, as you are in the flow of fresh experience.

All this comes not from changing our external world, but from cultivating our inner world through meditation and self-awareness. The openness, flexibility, fearlessness and effortlessness of beginner's mind is our natural state, hidden under layers of insecurity. Mindfulness allows us to return to our natural state—to be with life as it is, to be in flow with it. It's not a new-age practice or dogma. It's a return to our natural state of wisdom and awareness. We become sensible (*sense-able*), our experience is sensational, we are tuned in, we are in the flow of life.

Open-minded curiosity makes us smart

Beginner's mind seems like a paradox because we act as if we have no experience, yet we don't lose our experience. It's not like we become stupid or naïve and completely forget everything we've already learned to be true. For example, if we were to look at fire with beginner's mind, we would marvel at its beauty and wonder how it works, but we wouldn't reach out and touch the flame. The curiosity of beginner's mind makes us *more* intelligent, not less.

Pulitzer Prize-winning journalist and author Thomas Friedman coined the term 'curiosity quotient' to explain how people can learn about a subject that interests them, whether or not they possess a particularly high IQ. It might be expressed as the formula CQ + PQ > IQ, where CQ is 'curiosity quotient' and PQ is 'passion quotient'. When curiosity is paired with passion in the exploration of a subject of interest, Friedman believes, an individual may be able to acquire an amount of knowledge comparable to that of a person who is exceptionally intelligent.

Research bears out Friedman's proposition. A study by Sophie von Stumm, at the University of Edinburgh, has shown that while intelligence and effort are certainly important predictors of academic performance, curiosity is equally important. 'Curiosity is basically a hunger for exploration,' von Stumm says. 'If you're intellectually curious, you'll go home, you'll read the books. If you're perceptually curious, you might go travelling to foreign countries and try different foods.'

Of course, this has application not just in the academic world, but also in business and leadership. As von Stumm says, 'It's easy to hire someone who has done the job before and hence knows how to work the role. But it's far more interesting to identify those people who have the greatest potential for development, i.e. the curious ones.'[1] For leaders, the obvious implication is to always stay curious, no matter how much you think you know. As Albert Einstein said, 'The important thing is not to stop questioning. Curiosity has its own reason for existing.'

It should be noted that there's a subtle difference between being a 'lifelong learner' and cultivating beginner's mind. Beginner's mind is less about learning than about unlearning. It's less about *acquiring* knowledge than about *shedding* preconceptions. We begin to open up to the quality of the unknown. We begin to love that sense of not knowing. In beginner's mind, we recover our innocence while still maintaining access to our experience and wisdom. It is a beautiful and powerful combination.

Why do we resist beginner's mind and stay entrenched in expert's mind?

The undeniable nature of life is that everything is impermanent. Nothing stays the same. Everything that starts in time ends in time. Impermanence as a truth may feel easy to acknowledge, but at the heart of that truth is death—our own impermanence. The fact that death is inevitable creates a deep vulnerability and fear in us. To counteract this unease and discomfort, we desperately seek a sense of permanence by clinging to beliefs, opinions, ideas and concepts that stay stable, in thought at least, and give us the illusion of permanence. The subconscious reasoning is that if we can find no permanence in our external world, we can create permanence in our internal world through our beliefs and concepts.

As we learn from mindfulness, however, by trying to avoid discomfort we are avoiding the facts of life—the truth of things. The more we try to avoid pain, the more our capacity to deal with it decreases and the more things frighten us. In fact, we spend so much time trying to ward off discomfort that our natural courage and resilience are eroded. Strength comes from opening up and facing discomfort. And when we avoid what we fear, we shut down and lose the fresh open mind that is beginner's mind. We cling to the illusion of safely 'knowing' and being 'right'. Our curiosity dies.

Then arguing and blaming become habits. We develop a refusal to examine with open-minded and open-hearted curiosity. Instead, we become obsessed with protecting ourselves or ironically self-critical in an attempt to fix ourselves. None of this is learning, and beneath it all we are desperately seeking security. We're trying to create a sense of the known, a sense of safety and comfort.

The modern business world, with its endless innovation and rapid change, is showing us more than ever the truth of impermanence.

But the degree to which we have not found true peace with impermanence is the degree to which we will keep clinging to the status quo. We will keep hoping that one day things will slow down and become more stable, reliable and permanent. This is wishful and delusional thinking. The secret is to find deep peace and ease within the flow itself, within the total instability of life. This is beginner's mind. This is the safety that mindfulness offers us.

The fixation on seeing things as solid and permanent lends itself to endless judgements of others. 'I am honest, she is dishonest.' We make such judgements as though there was the possibility of pure honesty or dishonesty. But in beginner's mind we find a clearer way of seeing things. We see life as an endless series of moments in which we are honest or dishonest. Beneath our judgements we see our fear and we stay open, learning about our fear, learning about ourselves. Rather than falling asleep lulled by thoughts like 'I know exactly how this is...and always will be', we commit to staying awake. There is a deep humility and wisdom that arises from the cultivation of this kind of fresh, open, curious mind.

I was privileged to interview Jane Cay, Founder and Director of Birdsnest, an online fashion retailer in Australia. Jane has grown her company from five staff when it launched in 2008 to more than 100 employees in a town of fewer than 8000 people, and won a Great Place to Work award in the process. My colleague Charlotte Thaarup-Owen supported Jane and her team with a rigorous mindfulness program, and Jane shared with me how much it has helped them to shed fixed labels of each other and to work together with more kindness and compassion.

The program teaches people the neuroscience behind mindfulness and how it overcomes the 'reptilian brain', which is responsible for our fight, flight or freeze reactions. Her team jokingly refers to this as 'the crocodile' because when they learned about it one manager said, 'Jane, I can almost feel it like a crocodile inside my body, waving its tail, and then it just snaps!'

'I'm so excited that I now know how to tame the crocodile!' Jane affirmed. 'Conflicts still happen but we're able to get through awkward and defensive moments because inevitably someone will say, "Do you think the crocodile was let loose?" And we all laugh together as the tension is eased and we're able to be more open and friendly with each other.'

This openness has served them well. On one occasion a new hire didn't seem to be keeping pace with the others. Judgemental and hurtful labels like 'lazy' were being thrown around, which created a pack mentality that left the new employee on the outside. One of Jane's leaders stepped up and took responsibility for the situation, and completely turned it around. They dropped the labels and nurtured the new employee and she became a valued team member. 'Our leader was able to do that,' Jane said, 'because she recognised her crocodile. And breakthroughs like that are happening so much more as we all become more self-aware.'

When we are lost in the world of the crocodile we are filled with unpleasant feelings such as fear and anger. When we experience this discomfort we often believe it will last forever. But it never does, and so remembering that everything is impermanent can paradoxically help us to stay in flow. We realise that even our painful experiences will pass. Nothing ever stays the same, everything is shifting. Seeing the truth of this, we slowly but surely release our tight grip on life—the inner crocodile constantly fighting with life. Instead, we face it with openness and curiosity, embracing the vulnerability of our situation as a source of strength. This is beginner's mind.

Any time we try to push our experience away, it generates more fear and discomfort, shutting down and losing the very thing we all long for—a deep connection with life. We become less flexible, less alive, more brittle and fragile.

Falling asleep at the wheel

Resisting change is very limiting. It essentially cuts us off from our own wisdom, our natural state and the way life really is. And this prevents us from seeing new opportunities for growth and innovation. In this state, Challenge the Process as a leadership practice becomes fixated and aggressive. It becomes a desperate search for the next fixed thing, rather than a soft curiosity about possibility. Or it becomes a rejection of what is obviously needed for change — the very opposite of Challenge the Process.

It can also cause us to make knee-jerk, panicked decisions. Because of our low tolerance for discomfort, we desperately seek a quick-fix solution to make the discomfort go away. Our curiosity and learning die. The pain of our current reality finally starts waking us up, but we just want to make the pain go away so we lurch for the next false promise of certainty (a certainty that promises to protect us again from the endless flow and impermanence of things). Although it seems like we're actively engaged in trying to fix things, we're actually losing touch with reality, sort of 'falling asleep at the wheel'. And we often wake up a little too late. Even if we wake up in time, we're soon wasting effort in the fearful and delusional search for another fixed situation so we can fall back into comfortable numbness once again.

Most businesses readily acknowledge that they do not learn quickly and effectively from their mistakes. This is because they lack beginner's mind, constantly lurching from one fixed view to the next, while ignoring the greatest teachers of all: experience and reality.

Releasing bias and accepting reality

When we are not living mindfully, we often fall prey to two common cognitive biases: confirmation bias and sunk cost bias.

Confirmation bias, as you know, is the tendency to search for or interpret information that confirms our beliefs or hypotheses. We approach something with a preconceived notion, a fiercely held belief or opinion. We search only for evidence that confirms our preconceptions and validates what we believe to be true. If we find anything that appears to contradict our beliefs, we perform mental acrobatics to explain how the new information is false or irrelevant.

Business leaders are all too familiar with sunk cost bias: persisting with bad decisions irrationally because of investments already made that we cannot recover. We cling to such decisions to avoid the intense discomfort and vulnerability associated with admitting our plans or decisions are not working, that there are losses that cannot be recovered. We persist in an effort to prove ourselves right in spite of all the evidence.

Both of these biases show the expert's mind in action. The expert's mind appears to be secure in its knowledge but is actually deeply insecure. The desperate way it clings to its perceptions and conclusions is evidence of its fear of being wrong. It holds on tightly to its beliefs and 'knowledge' because that's what gives it the *illusion* of stability in an unstable world.

As research shows, mindfulness is a powerful tool for relinquishing our tight grip on the cognitive biases of the expert's mind. Andrew Hafenbrack of INSEAD examined the impact of mindfulness meditation on sunk cost bias. Our wandering minds, Hafenbrack and his team reasoned, lead us to dwell too much on the past and the future, which provides fuel for the sunk cost bias. They hypothesised that focusing more on the present would reduce the effects of the bias. Sure enough, the more mindful participants in the study proved to be less predisposed to sunk cost bias.

They staged three different experiments in which some groups were encouraged to let their minds wander before being asked to make a decision designed to evoke the sunk cost bias. Others were guided through a 15-minute mindfulness meditation session prior to being presented with the same decisions. Again the mindful group was significantly less likely to be influenced by the sunk cost bias — after only 15 minutes of meditation.[2]

In another study, researchers examined how mindfulness aids our decision-making processes. They discovered that, among other benefits, mindfulness may 'reduce confirmation bias and overconfidence, allow decision makers to better differentiate between relevant and irrelevant information, reduce reliance on stereotypes, help appreciate uncertainty and productively deal with it, and reduce illusory pattern detection. Furthermore, mindfulness is likely to facilitate resolving trade-offs and help effectively reconcile intuition with analysis, thereby reducing procrastination. Finally, mindful decision makers are more likely to learn to make better decisions over time because they are more open to feedback and less prone to misinterpret it by making self-serving attributions.'[3]

In short, mindfulness releases the grip of our expert's mind and its accompanying biases in order to operate from the openness and flexibility of beginner's mind.

The brain science of beginner's mind

For the past few centuries, the accepted paradigm in the scientific community has been that the brain is essentially fixed, hardwired, unchangeable. As the Spanish neuroanatomist Santiago Ramón y Cajal wrote, 'In the adult centers the nerve paths are something fixed, ended and immutable.' However, cutting-edge neuroscience is proving that our brains maintain the ability to rewire and change throughout our lives. Scientists have dubbed this ability 'neuroplasticity'. Sharon Begley explains in her book *Train Your Mind, Change Your Brain*: 'The brain can indeed be rewired. It can expand the area that is wired to move the fingers, forging new connections that underpin the dexterity of an accomplished violinist. It can activate long-dormant wires and run new cables like an electrician bringing an old house up to code, so that regions that once saw can instead feel or hear. It can quiet circuits that once crackled with the aberrant activity that characterizes depression and cut pathological connections that keep the brain in the oh-god-something-is-wrong state that marks obsessive-compulsive disorder. The adult brain, in short, retains much of the plasticity of the developing brain, including the power to repair damaged regions, to grow new neurons, to rezone regions that performed one task and have them assume a new task, to change the circuitry that weaves neurons into the networks that allow us to remember, feel, suffer, think, imagine and dream.'

One of the best tools scientists have used to stimulate neuroplasticity is — you guessed it — mindfulness meditation. Beginner's mind, as cultivated through mindfulness, can do more than simply help us see more clearly and make better decisions — it can literally rewire our brains.

To innovate, first create a safe learning environment

The organisations that will thrive in the modern technological world are those that can innovate, learn and adapt fastest. So how can leaders create a culture of innovation? How can they inspire people to constantly push the boundaries of the known, to enter the scary and risky territory of the unknown? How can they maintain that delicate balance between holding old ground and gaining new ground? How can they create new wins and open up new opportunities and markets without jeopardising their existing business? First, they must create a safe learning environment.

'Human spirit,' observes writer Bernard Beckett, 'is the ability to face the uncertainty of the future with curiosity and optimism. It is the belief that problems can be solved, differences resolved. It is a type of confidence. And it is fragile. It can be blackened by fear and superstition.' The fear of failure is poison in organisations. If you're not failing, you're not innovating.

The challenge is that cultures often give mixed messages. On the one hand, lip service is paid to innovation. On the other hand, leaders feel extreme pressure to 'get it right'. This makes them scared to try new things. Or, if they do try new things and fail, they easily fall into the blame game to take the pressure off themselves.

In a famous article, 'Teaching Smart People How to Learn', business theorist Chris Argyris, of Harvard Business School, explained why the smartest, most talented leaders are often those who are the least open to failure and capable of learning from failure. People profess to be open to learning, he explained, but their actions betray very different values, including:

- the desire to remain in unilateral control
- the goal of maximising 'winning' while minimising 'losing'
- the belief that negative feelings should be suppressed
- the desire to appear as rational as possible.

Argyris concluded that these values betray a profoundly defensive standpoint: a need to avoid uncomfortable feelings such as embarrassment, or a sense of inadequacy and failure. This 'closed-loop' reasoning illustrates why some find the process of open inquiry to be highly intimidating, and is specifically relevant to the actions of many of the best-educated and most highly skilled employees. As Agyris notes, 'Behind their high aspirations are an equally high fear of failure and a tendency to be ashamed when they don't live up to their high standards.'

These smart, talented leaders have brittle personalities because they are almost always successful at anything they take on. Excelling and succeeding is what they do, what they've always done. Which means that they've rarely, if ever, experienced the pain of failure. As Argyris put it, 'They've never developed the tolerance for feelings of failure or the skills to deal with those failures.' So when their strategies fail, they feel embarrassed and threatened, which turns into defensiveness and blaming anyone and everyone but themselves. Therefore, their ability to learn shuts down right when they need it most.

Defensive blaming is even more poisonous than fear of failure, and there is a clear correlation between the two. Mindful leaders can stop the blame game by creating a culture of compassionate accountability. Compassionate accountability isn't about finding someone or some factor to blame. It's simply about objectively analysing a situation with beginner's mind to learn from it. It's finding where team members may have contributed to a failure, but doing so compassionately, with an attitude of 'What can we learn from this?' rather than 'See what you did wrong?'

Learn to separate character from competence. There's a world of difference between a person who displays a lack of character or consciously violates values and a person who makes an innocent mistake based on a lack of knowledge or skill. A story told by Thomas Watson, the former CEO of IBM, illustrates this well. When an employee made a critical mistake that cost the company $600 000, Watson was asked if he was going to fire the employee.

He responded, 'No, I just spent $600 000 training him. Why would I want somebody else to hire his experience?'

That's the kind of culture that makes it emotionally safe to fail. Allowing people to innocently fail stops the blame game in its tracks; when people don't fear punishment for failure, they have no reason to blame anyone else. They are more inclined to learn rather than get defensive.

When I asked Paul Foster, Sales Director at George Weston Foods in Sydney, to explain how mindfulness has helped his ability to innovate, he said, 'Before engaging in a deeper mindfulness practice around my sense of self-worth, I was very quick to defend my ideas and my mistakes. I would also get reactive when people contributed ideas that conflicted with my own, instead of staying open and curious and asking them to elaborate on their ideas—an old pattern I still fall into if I am not mindful.

'Given the complexity of our business challenges, it is important to experiment in the market with new ideas and approaches. You can't pick the ideas that are going to work without giving them a go in real life. In order to do this, we run experiments that are safe to fail rather than fail-safe. This allows us to celebrate failure as a great learning experience without fear of a big loss.'

Shift from 'initiatives' to 'experiments'

In their book *The Leadership Challenge: How to Make Extraordinary Things Happen in Organizations*, Jim Kouzes and Barry Posner write, 'Leaders make risk safe, as paradoxical as that might sound. They turn experiments into learning opportunities. They don't define boldness solely in terms of go-for-broke, giant-leap projects. More often than not, they see change as starting small, using pilot projects, and gaining momentum. The vision may be grand and distant, but the way to reach it is by putting one foot in front of the other ... Of course, when you experiment, not everything works out as intended. There are mistakes and false starts. They are part of the process of innovation. What's critical, therefore, is that leaders promote learning from these experiences.'

The key word is 'experiment'. Leaders aren't used to thinking in terms of experiments. I often ask leaders to tell me how many experiments they currently have going. They typically say none, or they don't really even understand what I mean. But when I ask them how many *initiatives* they have going, that registers. They typically have five to ten 'initiatives' on the go at any given time. But the psychology of shifting from initiatives to experiments is profound, and the tangible effect is drastic.

With initiatives, we're stuck in the paradox of wanting to innovate but being fearful of making mistakes. We feel the pressure to maximise shareholder value and profitability. We use terms like 'best practices', 'benchmarking' and 'standards'. But there's nothing new in best practices; they're simply what has worked in the past. That's not innovation. Initiatives are often subject to confirmation bias and sunk cost bias because of the pressure leaders feel to make them work, even when the feedback tells them that something needs to shift. Initiatives often devolve into forced attempts to prove an idea or strategy right. Leaders feel a responsibility to make them succeed, which often leads to a refusal to recognise when they are not going well. Initiatives are also often an attempt to create certainty in an uncertain world. In this framework, there is no beginner's mind; there are only egos and experts who 'know' and then deny and defend when things don't turn out how they had predicted.

But consider the fundamental mindset difference that occurs when we reframe initiatives as experiments. In an experiment, when something goes wrong we don't immediately jump into blame and defensiveness mode. Experiments remove ego from the equation. We're simply observing and analysing with beginner's mind. The idea of an experiment isn't to force anything to succeed, but rather simply to learn. When experiments don't go as planned, we try to understand what this is telling us. Rather than imposing our ideas of what *should be,* we're letting the reality of the experiment tell us what actually *is*. We're playing around in a lab and watching what happens.

Speaking of a lab, what makes failure safe in experiments is boundaries. Just as we would set up safe boundaries in a science lab, we can create safe boundaries in business experiments. Don't do anything that has the potential to break your whole company. Make it safe to fail. Get really objective about the risk you're taking on. What's the worst thing that could possibly happen? Quantify it. Ask yourself if you can live with that failure. If not, change the parameters and boundaries. If so, then you can relax and move forward, accepting that the worst-case scenario is a real possibility. When that worst case happens, no one will be blamed or punished—we'll learn from it together. In fact, when we really understand the power of experimenting, we actually *reward* people for intelligent applications of failure. Getting the monkey of failure off your back gives you the space and mindset to learn.

When we venture into the world of the unknown, we can make all the projections we want. But the truth is that it's only through experimentation that reality can reveal itself to us. We can't work out in our mind what will happen in unknown territory. But that's exactly what we do with initiatives. We impose our expert's mind on possibility and claim to know what will happen. We create a strategy and then execute it with the expectation that everything will go as planned because we're the experts who know everything.

Life simply does not happen this way. The vast majority of scientific discoveries have come about by accident—playing around with variables in a lab and learning from what emerges. When you experiment, failures are nothing but opportunities to learn. And successes may just open up opportunities that you haven't seen before. Mario Testino said, 'My favorite words are possibilities, opportunities, and curiosity. I think if you are curious, you create opportunities, and then if you open the doors, you create possibilities.'

Overcoming the god complex

We've all experienced working with people who have varying degrees of the 'god complex', the unshakable belief that they can do no wrong, that they are infallible. I suppose we all demonstrate this complex, which is the most extreme manifestation of expert's mind, to one degree or another. The god complex is what we often engage in when we operate from a space of initiatives.

Economist Tim Harford gave a fantastic TED talk on the god complex, which is prevalent in business, economics, politics, medicine — virtually every field of human endeavour. In a staggeringly, incomprehensibly complex world, leaders and professionals are often absolutely convinced they understand how the world works and how to solve problems. Tim notes how hard and uncomfortable it is to admit our fallibility, 'In my own little world, I am a god, I understand everything. I do not want to have my conclusions tested.'

The way we solve problems is to use a problem-solving technique that works. As Tim put it, 'You show me a successful complex system, and I'll show you a system that has evolved through trial and error.' If you have a systematic way of determining what is working and what is not you can solve a complex problem.

The operative word is 'systematic'. Experimenting isn't simply throwing stuff up against the wall and seeing what sticks. It's being intelligent about the process. It's testing variables, quantifying the data and analysing the results. It's being a true scientist — which happens to be the essence of beginner's mind.

How to deal with complexity

In my experience of working with clients, I have found that, when faced with complex problems, leaders either freeze or react in a knee-jerk way. When I ask them to tell me how they propose to deal with complexity, they typically roll out an expert analysis solution, based on the view that it's possible to eliminate all risk through the intellect, to plan and do. Though it's certainly understandable, this is the worst possible way to deal with complexity. It's why we often stay stuck or learn too slowly to adapt to change.

Scholar and researcher David Snowden, the creator of the 'Cynefin framework' decision-making model for dealing with complexity, asserts that managers too often rely on familiar leadership approaches that work successfully in some circumstances but not in others. The reason these approaches fail when logically they should succeed is because of the assumption that there is a certain level of order and predictability in the world. As Snowden put it 'This assumption . . . encourages simplifications that are useful in ordered circumstances. Circumstances change, however, and as they become more complex, the simplifications can fail. Good leadership is not a one-size-fits-all proposition.'[4]

The most important thing a leader can do to deal with complexity is to cultivate beginner's mind. This enables experimentation and quick learning from experiments. We will never have all the answers and to assume that we do is incredibly dangerous. The best we can do is to explore the world around us and our circumstances with open-minded and open-hearted curiosity. We can try things and see what works, then quickly adjust when things don't work.

The underlying attribute of beginner's mind

Professor Jeff Dyer of Brigham Young University and Hal Gregersen of INSEAD surveyed more than 3000 executives and found that the most innovative leaders shared five mental traits:

1. **Associating**—connecting dots and recognising patterns across seemingly unrelated questions, problems or ideas

2. **Questioning**—asking 'what if' or 'why' and 'why not' questions that challenge the status quo and open up the bigger picture

3. **Observing**—closely observing details, particularly of people's behaviour

4. **Experimenting**—trying out new experiences and exploring new worlds

5. **Networking**—constantly meeting new people who have little in common with them, but from whom they can learn.[5]

While each of these traits is vital, underlying them, I believe, is an even deeper attribute that is the foundation and essence of beginner's mind: humility. Staying humble is the most important thing we can do as leaders. Humility keeps our ego in check and prevents us from calcifying into expert's mind. It keeps us open to feedback and learning.

It also prevents us from resting on our laurels and becoming prideful from our accomplishments. As Shunryu Suzuki said, 'In the beginner's mind there is no thought, "I have attained something." All self-centered thoughts limit our vast mind. When we have no thought of achievement, no thought of self, we are true beginners. Then we can really learn something. The beginner's mind is the mind of compassion. When our mind is compassionate, it is boundless.'

What leaders can achieve with the humility of beginner's mind truly is boundless. The new frontiers that await humanity lie beyond the reach of expert's mind and on the edges of beginner's mind. The attitude cultivated by the greatest leaders is expressed by Nikkyo Niwano, who, after a lifetime of mindfulness practice, said, 'I am beginning today. I am a lifetime beginner.'

Chapter 6

Empower others to shine

The greatest good you can do for another is not just to share your riches but to reveal to him his own.

Benjamin Disraeli

Several years ago a client called me and asked if I could book a session to teach a specific training module. I wasn't available on the day they wanted me to come, so we tried to find another day. We went back and forth on several dates and I wasn't available for any of them. Eventually I told them that one of my team members, Grant, was an expert on this module and that he could teach it instead of me. They told me, 'No, we want you.'

I put the phone down and was struck by how delighted I felt. I mindfully explored that emotion until I realised that I was delighted to have been chosen by the client over Grant. As soon as that realisation jumped out at me, I was floored by a second insight: a good leader would be *disappointed*, not delighted, that his team member hadn't been picked over him. A good leader would empower his team members to shine, rather than constantly trying to shine himself.

And then a third, even deeper insight revealed itself as I pondered on why I fell short in this regard as a leader: it all came down to insecurity. I needed to feel important. I needed to feel valued. And that feeling outweighed my imperative as a leader to help my team members shine, to boost their confidence and abilities, to empower them to be the best they could be.

That experience taught me a profound lesson on leadership that I'll never forget. Leaders can learn how to spend time with their direct reports. They can learn the importance of coaching. They can learn all the techniques and skills in the world for building people up. But if leaders are not *invested* in building and lifting their team members, their leadership efforts will be significantly hampered. People will feel their insincerity and ulterior motives and as a result will be less engaged.

Without addressing our own deeply held insecurities as leaders, we will never master the art of enabling and empowering others because we won't be fully invested in the process. In fact, whether we're conscious of it or not, whether we admit it to ourselves or not, we're invested in precisely the opposite. We're invested in letting others shine only to the extent that it doesn't outshine us. We want them to do just well enough to make us as leaders look good. We want our teams to perform well so we can get the praise and take the credit.

Mindfulness provides the insight and compassion through which we uncover our insecurities and then embrace and heal them so we can engage with others with unselfish intentions. The whole point of leadership isn't to get glory for ourselves, but rather to enable and inspire teams to accomplish what we could never accomplish alone. It is to empower others to bring out their best and realise their potential in the pursuit of a common goal. Our job as leaders is precisely to make others shine. People won't give their full effort if they don't feel like their leaders care about them and want them to grow. The more our leadership efforts are about us, the less effective we are.

Leadership is not a solo act. To make a meaningful contribution, we have to engage the efforts of others. Jim Kouzes and Barry Posner call this 'enabling others to act', which can be defined as (1) fostering collaboration by building trust and facilitating relationships, and (2) strengthening others by increasing self-determination and developing competence. Their research shows that when leaders enable others to act, their people are more than 30 per cent more engaged in their workplaces.

When I saw my deep-seated insecurities in relation to Grant and realised how I had failed as a leader, I started making changes. I asked myself, 'What can I do to empower Grant to the degree that it frightens me?' I wanted to push myself beyond my fears and to make him as free as possible—because in doing so, I knew I would set myself free from my own insecurities. Over the past couple of years I have helped Grant with certification programs that would enable him to leave my firm and become my competition, if he so chose. I did it because I knew any other choice is a choice for fear and smallness, a choice that would create suffering both for myself and for Grant. When we help our team members be the best they can be, without feeling threatened that they will shine brighter than us, they will give their best because they *want* to, rather than because it's expected of them.

The deeper mindsets required to mindfully enable others are generosity and compassion. They are the mental and emotional ground from which enabling springs naturally.

Cultivate generosity to release insecurities and empower people

Fear and greed are primary contributors to suffering. The insecurity I uncovered in my leadership was evidence of the fear and greed I carried in my heart. Human beings naturally tend toward a win–lose mentality, where we see everyone as separated from us and our losses as a gain for others, and vice versa. That 'what's in it for me' attitude that ignores everyone else is the basis for competition and conflict.

The acute awareness we develop from mindfulness practice reveals this tendency, while also giving us the tools to rise above it. When we are stuck in this win–lose scarcity mode, we can look at what is happening in our body and emotions with a degree of objective precision. In my case, for example, I feel an inner tightening and contraction—a sure sign of suffering. This sense gives us a clue that there is something there to explore.

A wonderful mindfulness practice for releasing that inner tightening and deep insecurity is *dana*, an ancient Pali word meaning generosity. Generosity opens us up and allows us to connect more fully with others. Mindfulness scholar Patrick Kearney explains: 'Dana is all about letting go. It's letting go of our clinging and learning to give freely. In monetary terms, if I can't let go of the change in my wallet, how can I let go of my inner obsessions and delusions? Dana is a practice by which we give externally in order to release internally. It's also a practice of love and compassion. It's about cultivating a social relationship.

'In the mindfulness tradition, to give someone a gift is an act of respect. You're saying, "You and I share the same values, the same project, and I want to be part of what you're part of." And if you accept a gift from someone, you're saying, "Yes, I welcome you on board." So dana originally had this broader, social connotation of building community. And internally it's all about letting go and cultivating love and compassion.'

When we operate from generosity, what we give returns to us. The more generous we are, the more our heart opens, the more joy we experience. Ultimately, dana is the cultivation of connection, from which grows happiness, cooperation and wellbeing.

This is far more than a feel-good philosophy—it has been demonstrated in multiple studies. Stephen G. Post, director of the Center for Medical Humanities, Compassionate Care and Bioethics at New York's Stony Brook University, says that generosity 'doles out several different happiness chemicals, including dopamine, endorphins that give people a sense of euphoria and oxytocin, which is associated with tranquility, serenity or inner peace'. He has dubbed this feeling 'giver's glow'. By viewing the brain using MRI technology during moments of generosity or selfless behaviour, scientists have found that even the thought of giving can engage this biological response.

One 2013 study published in the *American Journal of Public Health* found that giving time and assistance to others reduced the mortality risk tied to stress. Another study found that volunteerism reduced mortality rates more than exercising four times weekly and attending church regularly.

In a leadership context, generosity isn't about giving money or even volunteering time, but rather about giving of our cooperation, respect, attention, care and efforts to our colleagues, boss and direct reports. A leader moves from being an individual contributor to getting things done through others. The one consistent thing about great leaders is that they get the best out of others. They know leadership is not a solo endeavour. This is done through generosity of heart and spirit, generosity of sharing and supporting, of recognising the contributions of others.

Through generosity, we move from command and control mode to coaching and mentoring mode to bring out the gifts in others. We give people our time, undivided attention, insights and wisdom to help them become the best they can be. We learn to let go of control and to give people space, autonomy and responsibility to step up and contribute more.

Underlying the clinging to our work, power and ideas is the insecurity of not feeling like we're enough. When we practise generosity, we affirm to ourselves that we are enough. There is a gentle acceptance to generosity, an inner recognition that we are enough. We no longer need validation from the external world to prove our value. Generosity is the antidote to clinging and its accompanying suffering.

An old method for catching monkeys offers a good analogy. To make a monkey trap, you can hollow out a gourd, leaving an opening just large enough for a monkey's open hand to go through. Place a sweet treat inside the gourd, attach a vine to the gourd and stake the other end of the vine to the ground out of sight. A monkey will smell the treat inside, reach its hand in and grab it. When it tries to pull its hand out it finds its clenched hand is too big to fit back through the opening. It is trapped. All it has to do is let go of the treat, but it does not let go.

We too refuse to let go when we're caught up in greed. Generosity is the act of letting go. And as an old Zen saying puts it, 'It is not what we carry with us but what we let go that defines us.' Leaders who hog the limelight and claim all the glory, refusing to let go of their status, will find their prize is a piercing sense of emptiness—a kind of psychological poverty. In contrast, leaders who let go of their insecurities and generously give from their hearts to serve and uplift others will gain fulfilment for themselves and engagement from their team members.

The process of practising generosity is demanding. Generosity forces us to confront our fears of not having enough, not being seen, not being enough. We tell ourselves that if we let go of our scarcity mindset and try to help people, we will feel empty inside. People will try to take advantage of us, and we will end up losing. But nothing could be further from the truth. We receive what we give. Generosity is precisely how we gain what we hold most dear: peace, happiness and fulfilment—and ultimately a deep inner freedom from delusion and grasping.

Generosity is also a profound positive force for contribution, a core factor in finding meaning in our work. I once asked a group I was teaching, 'If you could earn double your salary for the next 10 years but would have to work at a job that made no positive contribution to anything or anyone, would you take the deal?' Predictably, they all said, 'No way!'

Despite our superficial fears of not having enough, our authentic selves love to contribute and make a difference for others. When leaders forget this, they violate this need in themselves and invite a deep sense of loss and meaninglessness into their system. This then feeds that sense of emptiness and insecurity, which keeps them in the cycle of being more of a taker than a giver. It's a trap crafted by our unexamined conditioning, but generosity is the key for escaping.

See the worthiness of others

Generosity is to see others as worthy of connection in your heart, and to make them feel worthy of connection and worthy of your attention. And when you connect with others on that level, they start seeing themselves as worthy as well. There's a transference of energy that makes them shine, not just because you're shining your light on them, but because their light begins to shine from within.

Psychologist Robert Rosenthal of Harvard University performed an experiment that showed the effect we can have on people when we see their inherent worthiness. The study was performed at an elementary school south of San Francisco. Rosenthal wanted to know what would happen if teachers were told that certain kids in their class had greater potential than others.

He gave the kids a standardised IQ test, but told teachers that it was a very special test from Harvard that could predict which kids had more innate academic talent than others and who would experience a dramatic growth in their IQ in coming years. After the kids took the test, he then randomly selected several children from each class. While there was nothing to distinguish these kids from the others, he told teachers that the test had predicted that this special group was about to enter a year of high achievement.

Rosenthal followed the students for two years and discovered that the teachers' expectations had a dramatic effect on the students' academic performance. 'If teachers had been led to expect greater gains in IQ,' he wrote, 'then increasingly, those kids gained more IQ.' After more research he found that expectations affect teachers' daily interactions with children in almost invisible ways. For example, students who are expected to succeed are given more time to answer questions, more specific feedback and more approval. Teachers also consistently touch, nod and smile at those kids more than those not predicted to succeed. In explaining the results, Rosenthal said, 'It's not magic, it's not mental telepathy. It's very likely these thousands of different ways of treating people in small ways every day.'

As leaders, we can positively affect our team members by seeing them through the eyes of generosity—seeing them as who they really are regardless of their behaviour. We help brighten their light by first *seeing* their light—even, perhaps especially, if they can't see it themselves.

Cultivate compassion to truly see people

Mindfulness practice is about cultivating both wisdom and compassion. The practices of values, focus, seeing clearly and putting sandals on (taking ownership) tend to develop our wisdom and insight. However, we also need to cultivate the heart-based practices associated with mindfulness and leadership. We need a balanced practice. Wisdom without compassion can be cold, aloof, indifferent. Compassion without wisdom can turn us into good-hearted fools. We need both to be our best selves, as well as to be the best leaders we can be.

It's easy to experience our own suffering and to strive to eliminate it. Compassion is cherishing other living beings and seeking to alleviate suffering not just in ourselves, but in everyone else around us. Mindful compassion in leadership is to wish for all your team members, boss and colleagues to be free of suffering, to thrive in their positions, to be happy and fulfilled, just as you wish for yourself. It is to truly see others and their struggles.

Johan Wikman, Chief Technology Officer at the language technology firm Appen, explains how mindfulness has made him much more sensitive to his feelings, which in turn has given him much more compassion for others. 'It helps me to really see the place they're operating from,' he said. 'What are their fears, what triggers are arising for them, what's driving their behaviour? A lot of times I'm able to understand people better than they understand themselves. Compassion gives me the curiosity to understand what makes people tick and how to motivate each individual. You can't have a rigid, uniform management style that you apply to everyone the same way. You have to be in tune with each person, and that's what compassion has given me.'

Johan's personal experience is now being confirmed by science. In one study, participants who engaged in cognitive-based compassion training improved their 'empathic accuracy', meaning their ability to accurately infer others' mental states from facial expressions.[1] The more leaders are in tune with their people, the greater empathy they can have for them, which leads to healthier, more compassionate relationships.

Compassion can be seen as a full-hearted embracing of the present. It is impossible to fully embrace life as it is, with all its pains and struggles, without compassion. It is a deep sensitising to the experience of life, and in that we come into more and more contact with our distress and with others'. This is the demanding side of compassion, and one of the reasons it's tough to practise.

If you've ever grieved deeply, you've probably noticed how people like to give advice and platitudes that are intended to give comfort but really don't help. This is because they often cannot hold their own distress in the face of ours so they try to fix the situation. Their 'fixing' is really an attempt to run from their own pain. All we really need in those moments is a good friend just to listen and stay connected while we grieve.

In fact, the word *compassion* itself comes from the Latin meaning 'to suffer with', or 'the act of suffering together'. There is a deep connectedness that happens when we witness the suffering in others and see how they are just like us in that suffering. As writer and theologian Katherine McHugh says, 'That healthy connection means that I will stand with you in your pain and you will stand with me in mine; and we will bear it together. We CAN bear it.' It is the deliberate choice to move toward connection and not to be dictated to by our fear and aversion. The fear keeps us running from the delusion that pain and loss could never happen to us, and this keeps us separate from life and from others, most especially when we most need connection.

This is why it is vital for leaders to cultivate mindfulness, equanimity and inner wellness, so we can face the more difficult things in others and ourselves without running. Our heart can stay open, and in that, healing and connection can occur. When we are compassionate we sense and connect with the other, and we feel their pain as if it was ours. We don't back away. If guidance is needed, we offer it. If listening is needed, we offer that. We surrender to the intelligence of watching and listening, and reality informs us of the next step as we act from our deepest wisdom. Leaders who can act from this place are a gift to their teams and stakeholders.

A practical exercise for developing compassion

Compassion dissolves barriers and helps us to reconnect with our lives and with others. Pema Chödrön uses an exercise to help us connect with others with greater equality and compassion. She writes: 'It is a simple human truth that everyone, just like you, wants to be happy and to avoid suffering. Just like you, everyone else wants to have friends, to be accepted and loved, to be respected and valued for their unique qualities, to be healthy and to feel comfortable with themselves. Just like you, no one else wants to be friendless and alone, to be looked down upon by others, to be sick, to feel inadequate and depressed.

'The equality practice is simply to remember this fact whenever you meet another person. You think, "Just like me, she wants to be happy; she doesn't want to suffer."

'…When we acknowledge our shared humanity with another person, we connect with them in a surprisingly intimate way. They become like family to us, and this helps dissolve our isolation and aloneness.'

Organisational hierarchies, as necessary as they are, can often become a barrier that keeps us from connecting. The implicit though unspoken belief is that the leaders at the top of the hierarchy are somehow better than those beneath them. By seeing others as having the same struggles, hopes and fears as ourselves, we cut through that disconnection. We may have different roles, but no one is inherently better or more valuable than anyone else. All of us have something unique and important to contribute.

Seeing people through the eyes of compassionate equality, we shed our impatience and our controlling mindset. We see ourselves as servants of our team members. We get in tune with our innate desire to help them experience joy and fulfilment.

Compassion fosters connection

When our hearts are closed, a sense of separateness governs our perceptions and behaviours. With that disconnectedness comes a tendency to view ourselves and others as objects that we use to achieve our goals. If people get in the way of our goals, we can very quickly close our hearts and go into avoidant, compliant or aggressive behaviour. And we further dehumanise them with labels like 'idiot' or 'selfish'. This habit of seeing and treating each other as objects is a cause of tremendous suffering, both at work and at home. When we are mere objects to each other, we can't see the hurt and confusion underlying poor behavioural choices, and neither can we see the light and beauty that is the essence of who we are. And our actions follow from that delusion.

One of the most extreme examples of this is the atrocity of genocide. In 1994 in Rwanda, Africa, for example, the Hutu majority slaughtered an estimated 1 million tribal Tutsis in 100 days. The term the Hutus used for the Tutsis was 'cockroaches'. On a plaque at the Rwandan Genocide Memorial in Kigali, Rwanda, is a profound quote: 'If you knew me and you really knew yourself, you would not have killed me.' All physical and emotional violence is based on seeing 'the other' as unreal, inhuman objects who are different and separate from us.

In the corporate world, we're certainly not killing each other, but the subtle violence that comes from dehumanising one another is an ever-present problem nonetheless. I have never met a client who does not have an enemy image of at least one person or group of people, whether suppliers, clients, colleagues, direct reports or a boss. Unfortunately, this is the norm; in fact, it's so normal that a part of me wonders if readers will think I'm overdramatising. It's natural in business because so much of what we do is task-driven, and we often view others as getting in the way of our completing of tasks. But we can never forget that underlying our tasks are relationships. And whether we like it or not, healthy relationships are central to long-term organisational success, effective leadership and our own happiness.

I once taught a course to a dysfunctional group of executives who had strong enemy images of each other. Team trust and cooperation were low. Two people in particular were locked in conflict. We were able to create a safe place to open up a dialogue. The first said, 'I don't cooperate with you because every time I share something with you, you take it over and do it yourself and cut me out of the loop.'

The second said, 'I take things over because I don't feel any cooperation from you. You don't work with me in the spirit of learning together, so I just do it myself.'

The first then said, 'The more you cut me out of the loop, the less inclined I am to share things with you and to cooperate.'

The second responded, 'And the less you share things with me, the more inclined I am to just do things myself.'

It was a vicious circle created by insecurities and miscommunications, which were firmly underpinned by each seeing the other as an object and enemy. By being open and honest with each other they saw that they were stuck in a self-defeating pattern. They made an agreement to change their relationship and get past the enemy images they were stuck in. Their story is no different from thousands of others played out in organisations every day. If we were to stop seeing each other as the enemy, we could help each other. In the light of compassion, our insecurities would dissolve and we would hold nothing back from each other.

Neil Thompson, the former CEO of the Velocity Frequent Flyer program for Virgin Australia, shared with me how his mindfulness practice has helped him in this regard. His job required that he work with people from a wide range of ethnic, cultural and linguistic backgrounds to create trusting relationships. 'Mindfulness has created a natural openness and natural empathy in me, which I think is the basis of compassion. I've learned to really understand where people are coming from, to really see and connect with them. Being mindful of their personal motivations and circumstances leads to incredible loyalty and trust, which in turn creates enduring relationships. It also helps me to resolve conflicts, because you can't do that unless you understand both sides equally well.'

I've made the human case for cooperation, and the business case is no less compelling. In July 2014 the professional services firm Deloitte Australia published a report entitled 'The Collaborative Economy' that shows how desperately cooperation is needed in organisations. 'Collaboration,' the report explains, 'is employees communicating and working together, building on each other's ideas to produce something new or do something differently. A collaborative organization unlocks the potential, capacity and knowledge of employees generating value and innovation and improving productivity in its workplace.'

Deloitte was asked by Google Australia to quantify the value of greater workplace collaboration, and their findings were astounding. The value of faster-growing, profitable Australian businesses with collaboration at their core was put at $46 billion. If companies were to make the most of opportunities to collaborate more, however, that number could be increased by $9.3 billion per year.

Companies that prioritise collaboration are:

- five times more likely to experience a considerable increase in employment
- twice as likely to be profitable
- twice as likely to outgrow competitors.[2]

Yet more than half of Australian businesses have no collaboration strategy. As a result they are missing out on significant benefits.

Technological systems and tools can aid cooperation, but more important is people who are willing to trust, connect and share. The collaboration technology needs goodwill to succeed, and for that to happen the leaders in the organisation need to foster a heart-connectedness with all stakeholders. We collaborate with those with whom we feel connected.

The fierce sword of compassion

Western culture teaches us to view compassion as soft and, frankly, weak and passive. We think that somehow being compassionate makes us spineless wimps who allow others to take advantage of us and who never take a stand. But nothing could be further from the truth. Compassion actually *enables* tough conversations because it allows us to conduct them without anger—to hold people accountable with purity of intent.

Compassion in action can actually look very direct and tough. Allowing people to break agreements and fail in their performance without holding them accountable isn't compassion at all—it's fear and avoidance. But when we hold people accountable compassionately, we do so with a complete absence of anger, which enables greater wisdom. We are not blaming or shaming—we are doing what is best for the individual and the organisation with love and honesty. We're seeing them with an understanding heart while saying what needs to be said, because dishonesty leads to broken trust.

Jack Kornfield puts it this way: 'Compassion is not foolish. It doesn't just go along with what others want so they don't feel bad. There is a yes in compassion, and there is also a no, said with the same courage of heart. No to abuse, no to violence, both personal and worldwide. The no is said not out of hate but out of unwavering care. It is the powerful no of leaving a destructive family, the agonizing no of allowing an addict to experience the consequences of his acts.'

Patrick Kearney adds: 'Compassion is the intention and action to end the suffering of people. You might think a person is suffering and your wisdom tells you that what this person needs is a dose of tough honesty that would snap them out of their suffering. So you apply the medicine.'

Karen Horsup, Group Marketing Manager at Midwich Limited, an electronic technologies firm in the UK, shared with me how she has had to learn fierce compassion. She used to avoid dealing with problems that needed to be faced. She would see situations and think, 'Someone should really speak to that person,' or 'Something should be done to fix this,' but she wouldn't act on it. The problems would then become much more difficult than had they been nipped in the bud.

She realised, however, that this approach was not helping people—that it was actually hindering their progress to not be completely honest. She learned that giving honest feedback, if done compassionately, can be the kindest thing we can do for people. She explained, 'It starts with being aware of the person and where they are in life. And sometimes they don't actually know how to move on or change. So those failures in performance or behaviour have to be addressed immediately. Everyone has their own life journey, and this is part of their journey. My job as a leader is to give them the opportunity to change, and to do so in a compassionate, fair, honest and open way. So I'm always very upfront and honest with people. Very often people will say to me, "You're quite straight talking." And I am, because I know the kindest choice is to actually honour people with honesty. To hold back is a fearful choice. It robs people of knowing what is really going on, where they really stand. To me, compassion and honesty belong together.'

With compassion, your intention is pure and your speech is clear and anger free. Your tough conversations are held with deep desire for the welfare and happiness of the other person—not to make yourself feel better or alleviate your feelings of insecurity or powerlessness. As Jane Cay from Birdsnest puts it, 'Tough love is about having compassion for people and creating trust so you can have a conversation that helps them become more conscious and aware of what's happening. They are then able to make the necessary changes and course correct. It's about creating a nurturing environment where people feel they can be vulnerable and authentic with each other. People have to know you care about them, and when they do they are so much more open to feedback.'

Nice or tough?

Jack Zenger and Joseph Folkman are leadership development experts who study what makes leadership work and what drives engagement. In a study analysing 30 661 leaders and their 160 576 employees at hundreds of companies around the world, they discovered two common approaches to leadership — what they call 'drivers' and 'enhancers'.

Drivers establish high standards of excellence, setting goals that make people stretch, and keeping people focused on meeting those goals. To put it simply, they tend to be task-driven. If you absolutely have to get something done, you want a driver at the helm. In contrast, enhancers tend to be more relationship-driven. They're in tune with the needs of others. They're great role models and coaches. They develop people and maintain trust.

When Zenger and Folkman asked people which approach was more likely to increase engagement, most respondents said that the enhancer approach was more effective. In fact, most leaders told them that being a 'nice guy' is the way to increase employee commitment. But the data tells a different story: 8.9 per cent of employees working for leaders judged as good drivers but poor enhancers rated themselves in the top 10 per cent in terms of engagement. But only 6.7 per cent of those working for leaders judged to be good enhancers but poor drivers scored in the top 10 per cent.

In other words, being either primarily nice or primarily tough is insufficient; both are needed to increase employee engagement. They reported that 68 per cent of employees who were working for leaders who were rated as 'effective enhancers and drivers' scored in the top

10 per cent regarding their 'overall satisfaction and engagement with the organization'.

They concluded, 'Leaders need to think in terms of "and" not "or". Leaders with highly engaged employees know how to demand a great deal from employees, but are also seen as considerate, trusting, collaborative and great developers of people.'[3]

The obvious bridge between these two approaches is mindful compassion, which enables us to be tough without being mean, nice without being lax. It helps drivers to see that people are more important than tasks, and it helps enhancers to see that truly seeing and loving people includes holding them accountable with direct honesty.

Asiri Senaratne learned from experience the importance of being both tough and nice. Asiri was used to being a tough leader in a high-performance, results-driven corporate finance job. But when that company was liquidated following the GFC, he took a job managing a call centre for a non-profit organisation, the Wheelchair and Disabled Association of Australia. The call centre was bleeding money fast and he was charged with turning it around quickly.

'I went in all guns blazing,' he said. 'I thought the old rule book was going to work: be the leader, stand up and say, "Today's the day things change. Today's the day we start to perform." Which is what worked for me in corporate finance.' Change proved to be much more difficult than he'd expected, however. With an average tenure of 15 years, all of the staff were highly resistant to change—and especially to his approach. Halfway through Asiri's first 'tough guy' speech, his entire leadership team walked out on him.

Asiri kept trying to be the tough guy for a couple months, but he made no headway. After reconnecting with his mindfulness practice, he realised he was operating from fear and anger. There was no compassion or kindness. He changed his approach to being more of a servant–leader. 'For the first time in my career,' he said, 'I was connecting with my team as people instead of as machines paid to deliver on tasks. I was working to improve their capability while also transforming the operation. I was being true to myself while being true to my values as a leader.'

What helped him bridge the gap was a moment of insight. 'I realised that my meditation practice was not integrated with my life,' he said. 'I was okay with being this guy who slammed his fist on the table and said, "These numbers aren't good enough, we need to change," and then going home and meditating. I had been led to believe that there was no place for compassion in leadership, because that was a weakness, or if not weakness, at least an ineffective way of getting things done.' Compassion, however, was the missing link that was preventing him from connecting with his team members. He began practising a more compassionate style of meditation and made a concerted effort to integrate that into his daily actions. He became a much more effective leader and helped to turn the call centre around.

Asiri's lesson deepened even further when he was next recruited to Commonwealth Bank, where he learned that his compassion practice had become fixated and inflexible. 'I came into the position as a warm and fuzzy, loving kindness, compassionate, understanding person. I had a very assertive, performance-driven general manager who thought I was great for a while, but he told me we had a job to do.'

Again, Asiri reflected mindfully and realised that, although his initial lesson was valuable, he still wasn't being flexible—a dead giveaway that he had lost his mindfulness. 'I was colouring my reality with a sort of fixed idea about compassion. It had actually become sort of a crutch.' He turned to a practice of developing a more clear-eyed, objective kind of awareness. It wasn't long before he started having the tough conversations that were needed. 'But with my new awareness, it came from a place of love,' he said. 'I was able to address situations immediately, before they got out of hand, and say that we needed to work together because the standards weren't being met.'

The balance was solidified when he was given the three most challenging performers to work with. 'With those individuals, soft acceptance wasn't what was needed,' he said. 'Change was required.

There was a directness and a bare clarity to my leadership style that had to be brought to the table very quickly. Mindfulness helped me separate my action from the emotion that I was associating with it, to look at the emotion really objectively. I would feel compassion for people and my heart would open up. But I was also aware enough to lay out my expectations. With every act of authenticity people's respect for me grew. When I saw them slipping into bad behaviours I was able to call them on it, but in such a way that they knew we were partners working together for their future.'

Striking the right balance between tough and nice is key, and as Asiri learned, compassion *and* clear insight through mindfulness is the path to that balance.

Empower people by setting clear agreements

During my years of leadership consulting I have met far too many leaders who are acting either from a fear-based niceness or with a heartless 'professional' aggression. They have not mastered mindful compassion, nor are they enabling others to act in a way that is truly empowering and uplifting. Fear-based niceness often leads to an amiable but chaotic, underperforming, even political team or organisation. Professional aggression often leads to burnout, alienation and disengagement.

When I've pushed these leaders to look deeper into why they are engaging in these self-defeating behaviours, I've discovered predictable patterns behind each style. The nice leaders are so fearful of disapproval or disconnection that they end up tolerating things they shouldn't. The aggressive leaders, on the other hand, impose stretch goal after stretch goal without much support, coaching or compassion.

Interestingly, in both cases the simplest starting point for breaking the cycle is setting clear agreements with people. Please note the use of the word 'agreement' rather than 'expectation'. People want to know what's expected of them. But rather than imposing edicts, a higher level is to create mutual agreements, both with direct reports and with colleagues. Take time to be awake and consciously upfront with people, not fearful or avoidant. We are not born to be slaves and when our boss takes the time to be mindful with expectations and agreements, it is deeply honouring.

Be clear on what you would like from the agreement. With clarity upfront, when it comes time for reward, recognition or fierce compassion, the relationship can be handled skilfully based on the mutual agreement. This eliminates the confusion of unspoken expectations and the hidden resentments that can create.

Agreements, as opposed to edicts and expectations, allow the nice leader to create genuine performance accountability without alienating people. They also allow the aggressive leader to add more compassion and support to the performance standards. Mutual agreements lend the courage of objective clarity to leader–team member relationships. Leaders don't have to push or dominate; they can simply point to the agreement. The nice leaders can more easily be fiercely compassionate, while the tough leaders can avoid the aggression and shaming and be more rational and compassionate.

In his book *Leadership and the One Minute Manager*, Ken Blanchard coined the term *seagull manager*, referring to managers who 'fly in, make a lot of noise, dump on everyone, then fly out'. The seagull management style can become a problem for both nice and tough leaders. The nice guy becomes a seagull because he panics when things fall apart. He dumps on people, then regrets it and goes back to being nice without accountability or true leadership. The tough guy swings back and forth from confronting and demanding to putting his head down and working hard himself. It's the same problem, just a different style.

I had a seagull manager phase when I was uncomfortable with clarifying expectations because it felt too 'leader-like'. I just wanted people to 'get it' without my having to spell out every detail. But what happens in this situation is that when people don't perform to our unset expectations, we panic and then swing the pendulum from avoidance clear across the spectrum to micro-managing. We swing back and forth between these two extremes, both of which are equally damaging.

In mindfulness terms, the avoidance style of management is aversion, while micro-managing is fear-based clinging. In either case, we create suffering for ourselves and others. And the solution for both is the same: creating mutual agreements and boundaries from the perspective of care and connection. For the avoidant seagull manager, setting clear boundaries makes people feel clear, empowered and motivated. For the micro-manager, having a mutual agreement in place allows you to let go and trust people more.

Fixing versus empowering

A painful experience taught me that there's a fundamental and drastic difference between fixing and empowering people. Years ago I was teaching a group of senior managers, who began our session by being very vocal about their belief that the program was a complete waste of time. Feeling defensive, I fell into a familiar conditioned pattern of mine: I became angry and critical. During the program I handed them back their 360 leadership assessment results, and all of their scores were really low. I was secretly delighted, because in a way it made me feel vindicated.

I really rubbed it in. I didn't use angry words, but in a nice, cool, 'professional' way I essentially conveyed the message that they were really 'broken' leaders who needed fixing. What ensued was the worst two days of my career. It was brutal and horrible. At the end of the session, most of the participants said the same thing about my program: 'That was the worst two training days of my life.'

A couple of days later the CEO dragged me in and asked me what I had done to these guys. I admitted that I got angry and had lost my bearings. Using deep compassion on myself, I saw that I had gotten really scared and that fear had come out as all-too-familiar resentment and anger. I then went to see a mindfulness mentor of mine. He asked me to consider the deeper mindset and energy that was behind my teaching of the course. I realised that once again I was seeing those leaders as broken people who needed to be fixed. And on an even deeper level, I saw them as needing to be fixed to prove my own self-worth.

It was all about me — the need to fix them to make me feel valued. I wasn't seeing their potential wholeness and goodness. I was talking to their brokenness — and that was really because I was speaking from a wounded and broken place in myself. It was projection, and unfortunately a projection going right back to my childhood. When you see people as deficient, a condescending energy is conveyed that repels people. And that repulsion wounds you even further and invariably supports more of the same pattern.

My mentor then invited me to take it a step further: to regard those senior managers as *my* teachers and to consider how that might change my energy and attitude. I met with them again a couple of months later. In the meantime, several of them had been actively canvassing the CEO to get rid of me as a consultant. That was the environment I walked into for another three-day training course.

I started the first day by being completely vulnerable and honest. I owned my baggage that had influenced our previous session. I admitted that I had behaved poorly. Instead of thinking of myself as the teacher with all the answers, I said, 'You guys are senior leaders. You know what you're doing. I'm just here to lay out a framework that may or may not be useful to you.' I was no longer operating from the attitude that I was there to fix or change anyone. My perspective was, 'These are not broken or deficient people. They're good people. What can *I* learn from *them*?'

The transformation was magical. After the two worst days of my career, this session was the best three days I've ever had. They were open and teachable. The energy was high. Breakthroughs were experienced. One manager came up to me after the session and said, 'The first two days you told us we were failing as leaders and we hated you for it. These three days you told us we were failing and we loved you for it. What did you do?'

I responded, 'I remembered you guys really care about the people you lead and that at your core you are brilliant and want to be brilliant more consistently. I was also honest with you. I owned my baggage. In doing that, you gave me permission to help and support you.' Most importantly, what I did was stop seeing them as broken and deficient, and instead I saw their wholeness and goodness. I saw the truth behind their attitudes: that they were scared their scores would threaten their career, just as I was scared that their attitude would affect mine. I was able to be mindfully compassionate and generous with them and to see them for whom they really were rather than as threatening enemy images. And as I did so I recovered my own wholeness and goodness.

As leaders, our job is not to fix people. If we have that attitude, we can be certain that we're seeing them as broken and therefore deficient. Nothing good ever comes from that view. Our job is to see the inherent goodness in people and to empower them to become what we see in them.

Part of this is not fixing things for people, but rather empowering them to solve problems for themselves. This brings out their natural talents and gives them the confidence to take on continually bigger challenges. Sergio Salvador, Google's Global Head of Gaming Partnerships, based in Singapore, told me that mindfulness has taught him this valuable lesson. Sergio provides regular, formal coaching for people on his team. Earlier in his career he had a strong tendency to step in and tell people exactly what they should do.

'One of the most significant things I've learned from mindfulness training is to drop that "I'm going to solve the problem for you" attitude, which is not helpful at all. I've learned to guide instead of dictate, to lightly touch a person's thought process here and there so they arrive at the best possible solution for themselves. It takes a lot of self-awareness and self-restraint for me, which I would not have without mindfulness.

'And many times people arrive at a solution that is completely the opposite of what I as a coach thought should be the right solution, but it's still more powerful because it's their own solution. If some of those solutions turn out to be wrong, it's part of the learning experience.

'Everyone is different and we all have our own unique reasons for doing things. I've learned that, even though I may have a really strong belief in doing something in a particular way for a particular reason, not everybody around me actually has to believe exactly the same thing that I do. So you have to help people discover their own reasons and methods. That gets them on board so much faster and easier than telling them what to do, or working with them on the basis of what's important to me. People are much more empowered when they have that sense of ownership.'

Turn on the light

Fear and delusion would have us believe that by empowering others to shine, our light is somehow dimmed. The reality is that the more we help others to shine, the brighter we all shine together.

The best leaders are those who confront their insecurities and take a whole-hearted approach to building and empowering others. They see the inherent greatness in others and they draw it out of them through generosity and compassion. With every interaction with people they ask themselves, 'What can I do in this moment to make others feel more powerful, competent and able to do more than they think they can?'

As you heal your own insecurities and become whole, your light begins to shine brighter. In turn, you ignite the light in others and enable and empower them to shine.

Chapter 7

Nourish others with love

Three things in human life are important: the first is to be kind; the second is to be kind; and the third is to be kind.

Henry James

I was once asked to help an underperforming senior manager 'get back on track'. In her boss's words, 'She is a real talent and has shown in the past that she can meet goals. But somehow in the last three months she is just off her game and I cannot seem to get her to open up about why.'

When I met the senior manager and discussed it with her, I very quickly realised the issue. She was ashamed to admit that she was just not receiving enough appreciation or recognition for the work she had been delivering, and the wind had gone out of her sails. 'I should be beyond this,' she said. 'High-performing people don't need praise, for goodness' sakes!'

I responded, 'It's not that you need praise. I think it's a deeper issue for you. It seems like you are feeling that your work is not making a positive difference, and the absence of feedback is heightening the sense that your work is meaningless.' I told her that these feelings were normal—the data shows just how prevalent they are in the corporate world. We need to feel our work matters. Like it or not, an essential part of leadership is to let people know they are important and appreciated, as well as how they are making a difference.

Every person in every position is doing work that matters. *They* matter. But too often they don't know how much they matter because they're rarely told. They look to their leaders for validation and often get the message, 'So what? Big deal. That's your job. That's what you're expected to do.' Leaders may not even be aware that that's the message they're sending, but it is real for people nonetheless. When a leader doesn't see and recognise their team members' contribution, they're actually breaking their spirits and creating an environment of loneliness and isolation.

None of us like being taken for granted. Jim Kouzes and Barry Posner asked thousands of people, 'Do you need encouragement to perform at your best?' Only about 50 per cent of respondents answered affirmatively. Those who said 'no' suggested 'they don't need encouragement' because they are 'adults' or 'professionals' who do their job well regardless of encouragement or recognition. However, when the question was changed to, 'When you get encouragement, does it help stimulate and sustain your performance?' almost 100 per cent of respondents said 'yes'. Clearly, we all have an inherent desire to be praised and recognised for our contributions.

An important leadership practice to cultivate is what Jim and Barry call 'Encourage the Heart', meaning to recognise contributions by showing appreciation for individual excellence, and to celebrate the values and victories by creating a spirit of community. The best leaders are always looking for ways to recognise and praise their people. They truly see their people and take notice of their contributions. They never take them for granted—and people can feel that from them.

The research shows that the least effective leaders use this leadership practice 23 per cent less often than those seen as moderately effective as leaders. The most effective leaders encourage the heart more

than 15 per cent more often than leaders reported as moderately effective, and about 50 per cent more often than those evaluated as least effective by their people. Furthermore, the most engaged people report that their leaders encourage the heart more than 30 per cent more frequently than the leaders of the least engaged people.

Research and consulting firm Towers Watson also provides stunning statistics showing how important appreciation is. According to their data:

- 7 per cent of people say their company is excellent at appreciating great work

- 12 per cent say they receive frequent appreciation for great work

- 56 per cent of senior management, 35 per cent of middle management and only 23 per cent of staff say their company is above average at appreciation

- 79 per cent cite a lack of appreciation as a key reason for leaving their jobs.

Clearly, appreciation is crucial to engagement. To be truly effective, however, encouraging the heart must be done authentically — praise and recognition must really come from the heart. People can smell inauthenticity a mile away. If a leader praises people mechanically, from the standpoint of a management technique or requisite checklist item, people won't internalise it or derive any satisfaction from it. In fact, they'll begin distrusting their manager, if only subconsciously.

Marion Furr, the director of Ministerial Business and Parliamentary Accountability in the Department of Health in the UK, shared with me how mindfulness has influenced her recognition for others. She said, 'I've often felt I was quite good at saying the right thing, so acknowledging people's contributions with words has come fairly easy for me. But what I've noticed with mindfulness is that my appreciation for others has become much more compassionate and authentic. It's not just about finding the right words — it's a genuine, heartfelt caring for people. And I find that I do it not just because it's a good practice that leads to results, but because it's something that I just want to do. It's something that arises within me quite naturally without needing any kind of training or technique around it. It just feels like the right contribution for me to make.'

Three heart-based mindfulness practices give us the awareness to see and connect with people more authentically than we ever have: lovingkindness, empathetic joy and gratitude.

Lovingkindness: the heart of mindfulness

As with compassion, we can have misguided perceptions and a limited understanding of love. Consider these dictionary definitions of love:

- a profoundly tender, passionate affection for another person
- a feeling of warm personal attachment or deep affection, as for a parent, child or friend
- sexual passion or desire
- a person toward whom love is felt; beloved person; sweetheart.

The ancient Pali word *metta* provides a more expansive definition, and one that is more easily applied in a work or community setting. Metta is a multifaceted word meaning lovingkindness, friendliness, goodwill, benevolence, fellowship, amity, concord, inoffensiveness and non-violence. It is a strong wish for the welfare and happiness of others, an altruistic love and friendliness that can be distinguished from self-interested amiability, affection, infatuation or lust. If romantic love can be compared to a flame, the lovingkindness of metta can be compared to an ever-giving fountain of goodness, concern and safety. Metta renounces bitterness, resentment and animosity and all social, religious, racial, political or economic barriers. It is unselfish in its application and universal in its scope.

For a leader, lovingkindness manifests as thinking of the welfare and happiness of the whole. It is to deeply and sincerely care about your people, to be emotionally invested in their progress and success. And it is to show how much you care about them by regularly and consistently expressing appreciation for their efforts. It doesn't mean to be a martyr and suffer for others. It is an invitation to extend love and kindness to all, including oneself.

Lovingkindness is the overarching context of all heart-based mindfulness practice. Without lovingkindness our mindfulness is not complete. It has a searching, ambitious, hard edge to it that in fact can create suffering for ourselves and others. The cultivation of a loving heart is a critical element of the practice. The cultivation of lovingkindness deeply affects the quality of our mindfulness, peace and happiness, as well as orienting us to the world differently. We develop a foundational mindset of heartfelt authenticity. From this place, nourishing others with appreciation, recognition and encouragement becomes very natural and authentic.

As a formal mindfulness practice, lovingkindness can be cultivated through metta meditation, in which we project benevolent feelings and wishes to ourselves, loved ones, friends, teachers, even strangers and enemies. The meditation can be stimulated:

1. *visually*, by envisioning the person we're focusing on being joyful

2. *through reflection*, by reflecting on the positive qualities of a person

3. *auditorily*, by repeating an internalised mantra, such as, 'May you be safe. May you be well. May you be peaceful and at ease. May you be happy.'

The purpose of each of these methods is to evoke a 'boundless warm-hearted feeling'. When the positive feeling arises, you can switch from the methods to the feeling, since the feeling is the primary focus. As you continually strengthen that feeling within yourself through cultivated practice over time, it spills over into your everyday life and you begin treating people with greater sensitivity, respect and kindness. Your heart opens up and you naturally start appreciating people more.

Through lovingkindness, I experienced a major transformation in my mindfulness practice. After years of meditation and disciplined mindfulness practice, I noticed that at times I was still bringing a subtle attitude of striving to the practice. Part of me was still reaching out to mindfulness as though a mindful state were something to achieve or attain. I would sometimes conceptualise and grasp for a presence that seemed always to be two seconds in the future.

That all changed during an intense period of lovingkindness practice at a silent mindfulness retreat. Lovingkindness really does not lend itself to goal drivenness. It's about surrender—a softening, not the hardening quality that comes with intense concentration and goal focus. I used to view lovingkindness as the poor cousin of insight meditation practice. This attitude kept me hard. In that retreat I finally let myself soften and really embrace a quality of soft kindness.

It was in the softening quality of lovingkindness that my striving dropped away and I became fully available—heart, body and mind—to reality as it was. It was a complete surrender, a releasing of the madness that there was anything in me to fix or change. And ironically in this I had a huge insight: that to be present, one needs to be soft within, to be available, kind and flowing, rather than rigid, hard or striving. It takes strength to be soft within because it opens us up to fully experiencing reality, to being deeply connected with life as it actually is, even at times courageously feeling all the pain that life has to offer.

Lovingkindness isn't something we achieve; it's something we discover was there all along. It's not something we go in search of; it's something we come home to. When we are really available to life as it is in the present moment, we can't be anything but loving and kind. Tapping into love is simply the recovery of our true selves.

After that retreat, I noticed an immediate difference in the quality of my life. Much to my surprise, I started feeling more connected, more alive and a whole lot happier (and I thought I was already pretty happy). It would show up in little things. For example, when I picked up my morning coffee I would really see the person serving me and would thank them kindly and authentically. I was really there, not rushing off two seconds or two hours ahead in my mind. My relationships with my team members also improved significantly. It is a rare event nowadays when I don't make a point of thanking them or acknowledging their efforts when they do great stuff (which is often). It's a radical change from my past behaviour, and it's easy to do.

Jane Cay, the founder of Birdsnest, shared with me how mindfulness has had a similar effect on her desire to recognise and appreciate others. 'When I practise mindfulness, my whole being bursts with gratitude for my life and those around me. And when I haven't practised for a few days I notice that I don't have that bursting feeling inside me, which has an effect on how I treat people. I'll think, "I want to go spread love among our team," but then I stifle that thought with other thoughts like, "Oh, they probably don't want to hear from me right now, they're all just doing their own thing." But when I've got that bursting feeling, I get in a zone and that energy comes out of me and I'm able to spread love without judging and shutting down my generous feelings.'

That is the gift of lovingkindness. Yet we often withhold love from each other because we're afraid of being vulnerable.

Love makes us stronger

We are all born with a natural tendency to love and care for others. But over time we learn to erect barriers and create coping mechanisms to protect ourselves from getting hurt. These barriers harden us and shut down our hearts, which makes opening ourselves up to vulnerability very challenging. We've come to believe that love, like compassion, means weakness. It's what allows us to be hurt. Surely, we think, we will be taken advantage of, laughed at or hurt if we are vulnerable. Ironically, protecting ourselves from our vulnerability hurts us more than derision or aggression from others. It keeps us feeling isolated and disconnected. We may feel safe and strong, but we are quite lonely in that 'safe' place, even in the company of others.

Once we learn that it takes strength to stay open and be authentic and kind, we find that the connection, community and joy that flow from this are far more valuable than the empty feeling that comes with the isolation we think gives us safety and strength. In that connected place we can see beyond our shallow judgements of others and begin to heal our teams, organisations and communities. We can also see through others' defence mechanisms, which no longer provoke us because our depth of understanding has increased so much.

Nicolette Rubinsztein, a director at UniSuper and SuperEd in Australia, told me a story of how mindfulness allowed her to open up to lovingkindness in the workplace. Nicolette is a naturally warm-hearted, compassionate, loving person, but in the corporate culture of her previous company she found that persona was viewed as soft and weak. The meetings were 'incredibly abrasive, like sparring the whole time'. Everyone tried to make themselves look good at the expense of others, to prove their superiority in order to climb the ranks.

To her dismay, she found herself acting against her values in order to fit in. In one particular situation, she denigrated a fellow employee—whom she actually really liked and respected—to her boss, and she immediately felt horrible about it. She justified it to herself as just part of the culture, what she had to do to get ahead. 'To this day,' she admitted, 'I still can't believe I did that. It was so at odds with who I am and what I believe in, and everything I now stand for about mindful leadership.'

She felt relieved and grateful when she moved on from the company and to a new position and found the culture much more supportive, connected and caring. When she first arrived she was invited to coffee with another general manager, whom she expected to be competitive, defensive and hostile. 'But she was anything but that,' Nicolette said. 'She was warm and inviting. It was such a revelation to me, the differences in culture. And that so resonated with who I am and how I want to work. It taught me that kindness leads to kindness. When you're treated like that you feel open to treating others in the same way.'

Nicolette now feels completely comfortable being openly loving and supportive in her job. As she put it, 'Mindfulness has given me the confidence to be kind and compassionate, to embrace that vulnerability.'

The benefits of lovingkindness are now being proven by science. One study at Stanford University showed that a regular seven-minute practice of metta meditation can increase social connectedness.[1] Researcher Barbara Fredrickson at the University of North Carolina at Chapel Hill found that metta meditation can help boost positive emotions and wellbeing in life, which then strengthens our inner resources to deal with challenges.[2] An EEG study by Richard J. Davidson showed that metta meditation literally changes the structure of the brain, including increasing subjects' ability to see things from another's perspective and moderating the amygdala, which is responsible for 'fight, flight or freeze' reactions.[3] Metta meditation has also been shown to lower reactions to inflammation and distress, both of which are associated with 'major depression, heart disease and diabetes'.[4]

Giving the best, bringing out the best

Great leaders bring out the very best in others. It is a core leadership competency that is more relevant than ever. Connection is an essential element of this. If you don't feel connected with your boss, how can they inspire you or push you beyond your limits? Have you ever worked with a boss who you know cares about you deeply, who sees the very best in you and brings out the best in you? Admittedly, such bosses are rare, but when you have one like that magic happens. If you want to be that kind of leader, cultivating lovingkindness is a wise choice.

Mindfulness teacher Steven Smith explained it to me this way: 'True lovingkindness is connection. Within that is healing. It is seeing and loving the entirety of another being, without picking and choosing which parts of him or her that you see and without any judgment, and feeling the essence, the core of the other just as they are. And that person knows it. They may not even intellectually know it, but they feel it. When you're really there and you're tuning into something, they feel riveted, they feel something going on. They feel that they're being looked at and accepted by you, even if they feel shame in themselves. The more present you are, the more caring you are and the greater effect you have on people. The best mentor is someone who cares for someone and helps them feel a better person.'

As we come home to ourselves and give ourselves that lovingkindness we long for, we discover within ourselves a limitless capacity to love. We find that the more love we give, the more we generate and the more we receive. Love truly is the source of our greatest strength, the quality that elicits the best and purest in us, that fortifies us against all hatred, negativity and challenges.

It's also a quality that enables us to elicit the best in others because it allows us to see the best in them. It improves our skills as a mentor more than any other factor because it gives us a heartfelt presence that becomes a real force for uplifting others.

Prakash NC, the regional HR director for the wireless communications company Rohde and Schwarz whose regional headquarters is in Singapore, has had plenty of opportunities to practise this in his role. Over the years he has found that more and more people come to him for mentoring and advice. Mindfulness, he says, has been key to helping people work through their challenges and issues.

'So much of it comes down to deeply listening to people with compassion and love and without judgement. Listening in and of itself is one of the most powerful things we can do to uplift others and make them feel important, because it's so rare that people really listen to us. So first and foremost, I give people my full, undivided attention. If I'm busy, I collect myself and take a deep breath to put myself into a space to listen.

'An accidental benefit of mindfulness for me has been deep insight and intuition into other people, a sensitivity to how people are feeling and what may be causing it. When I really listen to people I notice their energy and start seeing things they haven't even shared with me. I immediately know the deeper issues behind what they're actually telling me. People will come to me with a work issue and

I will intuitively feel to ask about their mother, or their family. I've had so many people say, "How did you know?"

'Sometimes I worry that it makes me appear eccentric, because while I'm talking to someone a vision comes up, or a voice, or a feeling. And I just follow it and ask people questions in a compassionate way. And I find that those intuitions are never wrong. But they don't come unless I really care about a person. I would say they are the product of love and caring.'

Equanimity: the foundation of lovingkindness

There is a direct and mutually beneficial relationship between equanimity and lovingkindness. Equanimity can be said to be the foundation of lovingkindness, as it gives us the inner strength to move past our barriers of fear and open ourselves up to being caring, kind and connected. Equanimity, cultivated over time through disciplined mindfulness and meditation practice, can be compared to diving down into the depths of the ocean. As you descend you are no longer pushed and pulled by the waves. As equanimity develops you become stronger and more accepting of all your feelings, pleasant and unpleasant. You experience a deep peace that is serenely unaffected by the endlessly shifting waves of life around you.

With equanimity comes a lovingkindness that is devoid of clinging. We serve without expectation of anything in return. Equanimity allows us to love freely and unconditionally. It releases our fear of vulnerability and opens the door to a deeper connection with others than we've ever felt before.

Lovingkindness also ensures a natural movement to empathetic joy.

Empathetic joy: authentic encouragement from the heart

Two words, one German and one Pali, with no English counterpart can reveal deep insights into leadership and relationships. The German word is *schadenfreude*, meaning pleasure taken in the misfortune of others. The Pali word *mudita* denotes the opposite: it means sympathetic or unselfish joy, or finding joy in the happiness, success and good fortune of others.

Schadenfreude springs from a deep sense of lack and insecurity in ourselves. It is a delusional layer covering our true nature of lovingkindness. It may seem fundamentally selfish and malicious, but underneath lies deep wounding; its selfishness and malice are but coping mechanisms, a desperate attempt to run from our own feelings of emptiness.

The cultivation of lovingkindness unleashes our natural capacity for delighting in other people's wellbeing and success. It is often compared to the attitude of a parent observing a growing child's accomplishments and successes. It is quite different from the pride that is often present in that observation, however. Mudita is a pure joy untainted by self-interest. At its deepest level, it extends universally to embrace all people, rather than being confined to close family and friends.

Mudita is a manifestation of 'putting sandals on' because it rejects all jealousy, envy and resentment. We have cultivated such a deep sense of wellbeing that we can carry it into the world, regardless of what the external environment (carpet) looks like. It's often easier for us to feel compassion for the suffering of others than to feel joy for their successes. This is particularly true when we are trapped in the scarcity mindset of believing that one person's gain means a loss for us. This is why this has been by far the hardest mindfulness practice for me.

I grew up believing that I needed to win and be better than others to be worthy of love. To prove to myself and others that I was worthy, my gain needed to come at the expense of others. Ironically, I sought to recover my sense of 'enoughness' in exactly the opposite way to that needed to achieve it. Much of my life was a delusion before I finally woke up to this. Old habits die hard, though, and this is still very much a work in progress requiring conscious, deliberate reminding and effort. So when I see another person working in my field gain fame or admiration, my default is still a pang of jealousy or ill will. But with the gift of mindfulness I can remind myself to look again, to see their joy and their success and to connect with that, instead of my habitual sense of lack. And slowly, with each remembrance, with each time I see it with love and joy, I rewire that old tape in my brain, and I become more and more filled with the inner wealth of 'enoughness'.

From a leadership perspective, if compassion means to 'suffer with', mudita, or empathetic joy, means to 'celebrate with'. It means being every bit as conscious of people's happiness as we are attuned to their suffering. It's not enough just to offer support when someone is grieving; we must also extend joy when they have succeeded.

After analysing compassion, love, equanimity and empathetic joy separately, it's important to recognise the relationship between each of them within the wholeness of an integrated practice. The Buddhist monk Nyanaponika Thera explains:

> Love imparts to equanimity its selflessness, its boundless nature and even its fervor…

> Compassion guards equanimity from falling into cold indifference and keeps it from indolent or selfish isolation. Until equanimity has reached perfection, compassion urges it to enter again and again into the battlefields of the world.

> Empathetic joy gives to equanimity the mild serenity that softens its stern appearance.

Gratitude: the gift that always comes back to us

We've discussed how the essence of mindfulness is heartfulness. Mindfulness opens our heart to love and connection; it also naturally produces a deep, profound and habitual attitude of gratitude. Mindfulness is about seeing reality as it is, and when we do so, we can't help but see the awe-inspiring beauty and miracles we're immersed in every moment of every day. In the spirit of gratitude we find the ordinary to be extraordinary.

What we all want above all else is a deep and lasting joy, a joy that doesn't depend on external circumstances. Gratitude is a catalyst for joy, because it allows us to see the good in every circumstance. It changes our attitudes, feelings and behaviours by changing our perception of events. Gratitude also allows us to see suffering in a different light.

Alchemists in ancient times sought to find what they called the philosopher's stone, a legendary substance capable of turning common metals into gold. It was said to be the elixir of life, endowed with the power to transform all things imperfect, diseased and corruptible into perfect, healthy, incorruptible and everlasting states. Such a transformational power exists in each one of us. Gratitude is the magic elixir that has the power to transform all negative thoughts, emotions, perceptions and experiences into positive, uplifting, joyful ones. When our thoughts are permeated with gratitude, we can't dwell on pain and sorrow.

In some Buddhist traditions, there's a prayer in which we ask the universe to bring us challenges and obstacles: 'May I be given the appropriate difficulties so that my heart can truly open with compassion.' Gratitude opens our heart to enable such a prayer, and it allows us to see the positive lessons that can be learned from our difficult experiences.

Through beginner's mind we see the world with fresh eyes and open clarity, with no judgements or knee-jerk reactions. We become present to our body, the people we interact with and the life we've been given. Gratitude is the default state for mindful people who see the grace and perfection beyond life's troubles. Gratitude and mindfulness feed one another: the more mindful we become, the more grateful we feel, and vice versa. Gratitude also helps us to see through the madness of consumerism and materialism. Living with a deep, inner sense of satisfaction, we no longer feel the need to find comfort and happiness in external things.

Doug Della Pietra, Director for Customer Service, Volunteers and Spiritual Care at Rochester General Hospital in Rochester, New York, explained to me how gratitude has benefited him as a leader. 'When I live from a place of gratitude I am more mindful, present and focused with my team members. For example, one very simple expression of gratitude that my team appreciates and that keeps me grounded in reality is thanking my team for showing up for work with a willing and positive attitude. While it's easy to take this for granted and chalk it up to the reward of the almighty paycheque, I can easily imagine the bind my organisation would be in if employees failed to show and engage with the positive spirit they do. So I am grateful and mindful of how much each employee adds value to and is critical to the organisation's work and mission.

'Recently, one of my team members told me that I am the best boss she's ever had. She said, "You're so thankful! Every email you write expresses appreciation. I've never had a boss with whom I am so fortunate to work!"

Honestly, her statement is very humbling. In fact, her words immediately led me to soul-search for the many ways in which I could have expressed more gratitude and taken others for granted less often. It's true that gratitude fosters more gratitude.'

Gratitude is a gift we give to others that always comes back to us in increased happiness. Put simply, showing gratitude makes us feel good. Psychologist Robert Emmons, author of *Thanks! How the New Science of Gratitude Can Make You Happier,* believes people who cultivate and practise gratitude are 25 per cent happier than those who do not. One study demonstrated the neurobiological basis of the pleasure that comes from gratitude. When we are appreciated, affirmed and rewarded for work we have done, specific circuits in the brain are activated and pleasure-inducing neurotransmitters and hormones are secreted in the brain. Recognising others trips the reward circuits in their brain, which reinforces the behaviours we want to see in them.[5]

In another study performed by Emmons and a colleague, they divided several hundred people into three groups. All agreed to keep a diary. The first group were asked to write down what they liked, good or bad; the second group were asked to write only about bad things; and the third group were asked to write only about good things they were thankful for. Follow-up assessments found that the participants who wrote about the things they were grateful for in their lives each day became more alert, more enthusiastic and optimistic and more energetic than those in the other two groups. They experienced less stress and less depression. Unlike those in the other groups, they found time to exercise throughout the study period. They also said they made progress toward personal goals.

Neuroscientist Alex Korb calls this effect 'the upward spiral' in his book *The Upward Spiral: Using Neuroscience to Reverse the Course of Depression, One Small Change at a Time*. According to his research, gratitude has the same biological effect as well-known and widely used antidepressant drugs that boost the neurotransmitter dopamine, such as Wellbutrin. He writes, 'The benefits of gratitude start with the dopamine system, because feeling grateful activates the brain stem region that produces dopamine. Additionally, gratitude toward others increases activity in social dopamine circuits, which makes social interactions more enjoyable.'

Additionally, when we think of things for which we're grateful, our brain is forced to focus on the positive aspects of our life, which increases serotonin production in the anterior cingulate cortex in the same way that Prozac does. Korb explains: 'It's not finding gratitude that matters most; it's remembering to look in the first place. Remembering to be grateful is a form of emotional intelligence. One study found that it actually affected neuron density in both the ventromedial and lateral prefrontal cortex. These density changes suggest that as emotional intelligence increases, the neurons in these areas become more efficient. With higher emotional intelligence, it simply takes less effort to be grateful.'

Gratitude fosters cooperation within organisations. Researchers Monica Bartlett and David DeSteno at Northeastern University, Boston, conducted a study that showed that gratitude breeds gratitude. They brought together a group of students in a room, supposedly to participate in a study, but before the students were called, their computers were sabotaged. The student would walk into the room, sit at the computer and realise it wasn't working, then another student would step forward and offer to help fix it. Grateful students were then more likely to volunteer to help another person in the experiments that followed, even if they did not know the person and the task was unrelated to what they were doing.

For leaders, gratitude is a catalyst for recognition. It makes us constantly look for the good in people and feeds our desire to share our gratitude for a job well done. It is a light we carry with us that people are drawn to because they feel good about themselves when they are around us.

The reality, however, is that we are biologically hardwired to see the negative in people and circumstances. Therefore, gratitude is a state and a habit that must be consciously cultivated.

Overcoming our hardwired disposition to negativity

In chapter 1, I mentioned Rick Hanson and his work on negativity bias. In his book *Hardwiring Happiness: The New Brain Science of Contentment, Calm, and Confidence*, he explains how to help our ancestors survive in harsh conditions, the brain evolved to look for bad news, overreact to it and fast-track negative experiences into emotional memory. In effect, our brain is like Velcro for the negative but Teflon for the positive. As our ancestors evolved, avoiding 'sticks' was more important than getting 'carrots', which means we learned to:

- scan for bad news
- over-focus on it, losing sight of the whole
- overreact to it
- install it rapidly in implicit memory
- sensitise the brain to the negative
- create vicious cycles.

In effect, the brain is good at learning from bad experiences but bad at learning from good ones, even though learning from good experiences is the primary way to build up psychological resources.

Rick teaches a concept called 'positive neuroplasticity', centred on our ability to rewire our brains to focus more on positives than negatives to increase our awareness of and capacity for gratitude. The mindfulness exercise to reverse this tendency is as follows:

1. **Have a beneficial experience.** The first step is to become more aware of things for which we're grateful. For example, you could be driving in your car on a normal day and take particular notice of beautiful clouds in the sky. Or perhaps your child wrote you a note. Whatever it is, move it into the foreground of your conscious awareness and focus exclusively on it.

2. **Enrich the experience.** This means sustaining the experience and really feeling it in your body. Let it wash over you. Revel in the positive feelings. Consciously and actively intensify the feelings by opening up your mind to the experience. Engage with multiple aspects of the experience, including perception and emotion.

3. **Absorb the experience.** Receive it by imagining and/or sensing it really sinking in. The key to rewiring our brains, Rick says, is to hold on to our feelings of gratitude for positive experiences for a minimum of 20 seconds. While enriching makes experiences more powerful, absorbing makes memory systems more receptive by priming and sensitising them. Without turning passing mental states into an enduring neural structure there is no learning and no functional change in the brain.

Again, the relevance for leaders is that it's not natural for us to notice the positive things people do and to be encouraging. We're working against our biological programming. By expressing appreciation, we are supporting not only our people but also our own development. We're reorienting and rewiring our mind to focus on the positive. Essentially, conscious gratitude reprograms our mind for greater happiness.

The encouragement ratio: bringing out the best in people

A casual 'thank you' every once in a while doesn't cut it. Effective leaders really give time and effort to appreciating their people. They go out of their way to make a big deal out of recognition. As it turns out, not only are sincere, heartfelt praise and encouragement important, but the frequency with which they are shared with others matters a great deal too.

Researcher Emily Heaphy and consultant Marcial Losada examined the effectiveness of 60 leadership teams at a large information processing company. 'Effectiveness' was measured according to financial performance, customer satisfaction ratings and 360-degree feedback ratings of the team members. They found that the factor that produced the greatest difference between the most and least successful teams was the ratio of positive comments ('I agree with that', for instance, or 'That's a terrific idea') to negative comments ('I don't agree with you' or 'We shouldn't even consider doing that') that the participants made to one another. (It should be pointed out that negative comments could go as far as sarcastic or disparaging remarks.) The average ratio for the highest-performing teams was 5.6 (that is, nearly six positive comments for every negative one). The medium-performance teams averaged 1.9 (almost twice as many positive comments as negative ones). But the average for the low-performing teams, at 0.36 to 1, was almost three negative comments for every positive one.[6]

It could be said that gratitude, appreciation, recognition and encouragement are the oil that greases the wheels of organisations. They increase trust and foster cooperation. Simply put, we feel better about ourselves, we perform better, and we enjoy working more with people who encourage us and recognise our contributions.

Using recognition to reinforce values and improve behaviour

Encouragement and recognition are about more than just making people feel good. They are how leaders reinforce core organisational values and standards of behaviour and motivate people to achieve shared goals. Values, standards and goals provide the context for effective recognition. They tell people, 'This is what is important here.' When consistently reinforced with recognition, people start to believe that leaders are serious about them.

For more than two centuries, Adam Smith's ideas have shaped how economists think about human beings and the choices we make. His basic theory is that we are self-interested and we make choices that we expect will create maximum utility for us. The problem with this simplistic view is that it discounts the role emotion plays in decision making. We're now finding that economists' predictions about human choices haven't matched up with what we actually choose.

Daniel Kahneman, a professor emeritus of psychology at Princeton, changed how we think about decision making. In 2002 he won the Nobel Prize in Economics for pointing out something that now seems quite obvious: 'Utility cannot be divorced from emotion, and emotion is triggered by changes. A theory of choice that completely ignores feelings such as the pain of losses and the regret of mistakes is not only descriptively unrealistic, it also leads to prescriptions that do not maximize the utility of outcomes as they are actually experienced.'[7] In other words, human beings are, in fact, utility maximisers, but emotions are very much part of the equation. This explains, for example, why many of us choose to drive the cars we do when more 'sensible' choices are available at a lower cost.

The application for leaders is that employees make economic choices every day, even if we don't think of it that way. They choose where to invest their attention and discretionary energy. They choose whether or not they owe loyalty to their leaders. How Kahneman might explain his insight is that (1) employees do what makes them feel good, and avoid what makes them feel bad, therefore (2) as a leader your greatest source of power is your ability to influence the way your people feel.

If you expect people to do their jobs because the position and paycheque should be reward enough, you'll find that engagement plummets. Expectations alone do not motivate people to greatness. Expectation-based leadership creates a scenario in which people give the minimum amount of time and effort required to not get fired. If you want to bring out the best in people, you must recognise, appreciate and encourage them.

Flowering from within

Within every individual is potential greatness, but over time people learn to protect against the vulnerability needed to reveal their greatness. They have been hurt too many times to feel safe to shine their light. They feel like they are not enough. This manifests in many forms, from antagonistic defensiveness to simply giving minimal effort. But through lovingkindness, empathetic joy and gratitude, leaders can unleash the greatness in their people.

You will be amazed by what people can do when they feel safe, valued and important. By watering the ground of their being with sincere, heartfelt praise and encouragement, you will be able to watch them flower from within. You will bring out the best in them. Your organisation will perform better than it ever has. And the greatest reward of all is the feeling of peace, warmth and happiness you will create within yourself.

Chapter 8

Transforming for good

There isn't enough darkness in all the world to snuff out the light of one little candle.

Gautama Buddha

The world is desperate for great leadership—more specifically, for mindful leadership. Suffering abounds in our personal and professional lives. The greatest opportunity for leaders is not to accomplish monumental tasks but rather to alleviate suffering. Given that we spend a significant part of our lives at work, organisational leaders in particular can make a profound difference—and at a much deeper level than we typically think.

When we see people as whole human beings, with private struggles and secret dreams, personal demons and public virtues, deep wounds and unique gifts, and, above all, a deep yearning to really *matter*, we begin to lead them as though they really count and to draw out their whole selves. We see that a job can be about more than salary—it can be a source of meaning. We see that the core purpose of all economic activity is not solely to produce economic wealth, but also to produce greater happiness, peace, wisdom and understanding. We see that we cannot separate our economic life from our personal life and our relationships, that everything we do is part of an integrated whole and creates a net effect in happiness or suffering.

We also see that the practices required for great leadership are precisely those that make us great human beings. The ultimate objective of mindful leadership is not some goal 'out there'; rather, it is to become the best kind of person who creates and supports the best kind of organisations. And the fruit of this work is a profound inner wellbeing—the very essence of what we're all striving for. Through mindfulness, we discover that what we've been searching for all our lives has been inside us all along. At its essence, mindful leadership is about coming home to ourselves, and then inviting, influencing, serving and supporting others to do the same.

The paradox of mindfulness is that accessing and living from our true, natural, most authentic self requires practice. It's available to us in any given moment, but disciplined practice is needed to help us see that. Marion Furr from the UK Department of Health puts it like this: 'I think of mindfulness in the same way as we do about our bodies. If you give your body the right elements every day it will perform well, and if you don't, it breaks down. And you have to give it what it needs even if you don't like it or if you don't believe it. It responds based on what you feed it and how you treat it. Our minds are no different. If you feed your mind a steady, healthy diet of mindfulness practice, you become more aware and capable—your mind just functions better.'

Inner transformation, then, is a lifelong commitment. Having said that, the reality is that with mindfulness practice we can make quantum leaps in our levels of understanding and self-regulation as we uncover the core issues sabotaging our best intentions. Superficial techniques may give us small, linear improvements, but mindfulness opens the door to exponential growth.

This work takes strength. Cultivating mindfulness is far more than just becoming calmer and clearer. It's about embracing our whole lives and coming to terms with the parts in ourselves we would rather avoid or run from. As we become whole again, the inner arguments, self-criticism and plea-bargaining slowly dissipate. We come to accept the sweet and the sad, the painful and the pleasant, with an inner grace. And in that acceptance we open ourselves to life so much more deeply.

I have been lucky enough to see the fruits of mindfulness practice in my parenting life. As I write this, my first two children are 18 and 17, and I have a four-month-old son. After 22 years of mindfulness practice I see how the way I relate to my new baby is utterly different from how I related to my first two children when they were babies. Indeed I realise I actually missed their time as babies. I was impatiently waiting to relate to them as 'people' and missed their miraculous time as infants and toddlers.

With my new little boy I can truly enjoy the wonder of his discoveries. Every day he discovers something new, from seeing that his hand belongs to him to staring at a pattern on a shirt in utter amazement. I see beginner's mind in action and I find myself easily re-entering beginner's mind with him and feeling a new fascination with life in the smallest things. My time with him has become a world of wonder and magic. When my first two kids were his age my practice was still immature, and I feel a tremendous sadness that I was not able to embrace that quality in them too. Equally, I feel tremendous gratitude that I can connect with them in a profound way as they grow into young adults. I can see clearly how my inner healing has paved the way for them to work through some of their own struggles with a parent to share it all with safely. As I have learned to accept and hold my own sadness and pain with more kindness, so I can hold theirs too.

Mindfulness practice has given me the priceless gift of learning to stop running from my full humanness. Part of my motivation in writing this book was my wish for all human beings to be able to embrace the whole of life. As I write this, my practice is still far from perfect. Some days I still run from pain (usually toward the fridge or TV), and even that is okay—part of the journey, the perfect imperfection of being a human being. I've learned to embrace it with kindness, without rationalisation or inner self-flagellation, which serve only to shut us down and arrest our development. This kind and full embracing of ourselves and our lives helps us develop an inner strength to face the truth of things. And as was once beautifully written, 'The truth will set you free.'

I have seen this quality in so many of the leaders I have had the privilege to work with personally and to interview for this book. They all have a common quality of humility, a shared knowing that they are still flawed beginners and will likely always be flawed. As paradoxical as it might sound, this is part of what makes them so inspiring—their honesty with themselves makes them so much easier to connect with, to laugh with and to trust. They embody that quality of authenticity we all long for in leaders. They don't hold on so tightly to a fixed image of themselves. They can embrace a bigger picture and carry themselves a little more lightly than the average person, and perhaps laugh at themselves a little more.

This unshakable personal freedom is the ultimate promise of mindfulness. Beyond the tangible, measurable benefits, mindfulness opens our heart to things as they are in the present moment. We drop our resistance to and battles with reality. In the present moment, we awaken to the love, joy and peace that are our essence. We drop the delusion of separation and connect with people on a deeper level than we ever have. No longer bound by our mentally created stories, we accept the mystery of life and cultivate an inner harmony that can be found in no other way.

Overcoming 'immunity to change'

Being able to see and embrace our whole humanness, including our fragility and darkness, is critical because of a phenomenon dubbed 'immunity to change' by Harvard psychologist Robert Kegan. Kegan believes desire and motivation aren't enough to change — even when it's literally a matter of life or death — because of internal mechanisms that make us highly resistant to change. For example, one landmark study showed that even after suffering a stroke or developing coronary heart disease, only one in seven patients will change their smoking, exercise or dietary habits.[1]

We resist change, Kegan says, because our mind acts as a sort of immune system to protect us from the psychological trauma and danger that sudden and drastic changes can bring. Unfortunately, this same system meant to protect us from negative changes can also prevent us from making significant positive changes. Change can trigger our defence mechanisms, thus sabotaging our efforts before we've even begun. Despite our best conscious efforts, there are deep subconscious forces at play in our transformational journey.

One of our strongest sources of resistance to change, according to Kegan's research, is our firmly entrenched self-identity. For example, when heart disease patients stop taking prescription drugs, one reason they cite is because it makes them feel old. One patient told Kegan that the reason he stopped taking his medication was because 'I'm 58 years old and am in the prime of my life. I'm not an old man with one foot in the grave.' Taking a daily pill threatened his identity as a healthy and younger man.

Mindfulness is the single greatest antidote to identity-based resistance because the practice teaches and enables us to let go of our self-identity and truly know ourselves, our self-awareness growing as we observe the changes throughout our lives. Through mindfulness, we no longer identify ourselves in rigid and inflexible ways; we merely observe different phases and states as they come and go. We no longer feel the need to cling to transient, impermanent states and intangible thoughts in order to find security. We develop a flexibility and malleability that can come in no other way. We find a peace that transcends all thoughts, concepts, identities and conditions.

There is more to behaviour change than meets the eye

We often view behaviour change as a technique or an intellectual knowing. We can buy into the attractive idea that intellectual understanding equals transformation. I must confess I wish that were the case—it would be a whole easier than the reality! Sadly, this is one of the reasons so many people are cynical about corporate training: intellectual understanding is not even close to enough, and it delivers nothing in the way of real results. It's a little like thinking that an understanding of how to exercise will make you fit. Again, wouldn't that be nice? The process is a lot grittier than that and there are some important aspects to remember, including the following:

1. Keep it simple and work on one thing at a time.

2. Know that when you are working through serious discomfort you are almost certainly making real progress (just like getting fit).

One step at a time

I sometimes joke with my clients that I am going to insult them intellectually while radically challenging them on an emotional and behavioural level. It can feel intellectually insulting because transformational practice sounds so simple. For example, I could say, 'Sitting meditation is the simple act of being present and paying attention to your breath as an anchor. Do it and it will change your life.' That sounds like an implausible, ridiculous claim. What is missing from this simple instruction is the specifics of what happens when you actually do this practice. Sitting still is very challenging and the process itself is an incredible teacher in so many ways. The process itself will transform you as it teaches you about distress intolerance and your relationship with yourself and your mind.

Secondly, given that transformational behaviour change is so demanding on so many levels, the key is to take one step at a time and focus on one behaviour at a time. You'll find that when one thing changes through mindfulness work, it impacts a host of other issues in your life as your self-awareness broadens and deepens.

Think of it this way: If you were to change more than one thing in your golf swing or swimming stroke, how well would that work? Anyone who has ever tried it knows it doesn't work. Trying to change two behaviours at the same time is too confusing for the mind—there are far too many moving parts for us to focus on simultaneously. You focus intently on one aspect of your swing or stroke until you master that, then you move on to the next thing.

Discomfort = Progress

When we take on a behavioural change, we are challenging deeply held habits. Many of those habits (especially the dysfunctional ones) developed as a means to shut down difficult feelings. As a simple example, overeating is usually associated with numbing feelings of anxiety, and if we stop overeating we are left to face and deal with the anxiety. If we cannot tolerate the anxiety, we head back to the fridge to indulge in something that will numb it.

In other words, when we embrace a healthy behaviour change we are certain to bump into mild to extreme discomfort and often uncover deeper issues that are driving the dysfunctional behaviour.

I watched this process with a client of mine, an executive at a global pharmaceutical company. She was crushed when she received poor scores on a 360 leadership assessment for the component 'Follows through on promises and commitments'. Another consultant advised her to attend a time management seminar to learn how to manage her time better.

I wanted to dig deeper to discover the subconscious patterning behind what was happening—to find the root cause. So I asked her, 'What is the core behaviour that results in your falling short of your promises and commitments?' She responded that she had too much to do. 'And how did that arise?' She admitted that she said yes to people too often. As she put it, 'I overcommit.' I then asked, 'Why do you say yes when you know in the back of your mind you can't deliver?'

What eventually emerged was that she was hooked on approval. When she said yes to people, they were happy with her and she felt good about herself. And she was addicted to that feeling. But now came the real discovery—the deeper why behind the behaviour. She explained that her parents were blue-collar immigrant workers. They had had a hard life and wanted her to be a professional and have a better life. They had chosen her career for her—with the best intentions. Every time she voiced a desire to do something different, she felt like they disapproved and withdrew their love. The message she got was that she needed to be who her parents wanted her to be. Unfortunately, from this she learned that her authentic self was not enough. She needed to be someone other than herself, and that inner pain was compensated for by the approval of others.

She was now conscious of the core reason why she was overcommitting, but she still had to deal with the behaviour and erase the patterning. I told her, 'When you say no to people, your past wounding will be aroused. When that happens, the first thing you need to do is take a deep breath and feel your body. Ground yourself. Ask yourself if you can deliver on this request. If not, say so. Then prepare yourself for "cold turkey" withdrawal—your "drug" of approval won't be there to compensate for the inner pain. It will not be fun. You'll get sweaty and feel distressed. This is when you need to manage yourself by being mindful of your body and the pain. Slowly but surely the discomfort will evaporate. And when you succeed, really acknowledge and celebrate that success. You are doing something incredibly supportive for yourself and others; you are reaffirming your value and living in deeper integrity with others. Acknowledging your positive progress is another crucial component of the process, it helps rewire the brain and gives you the fuel to keep going in the face of discomfort.

By staying grounded in an awareness of her body, embracing the pain and the good when she succeeds, she is freeing herself from these habitual patterns. More importantly, the self-awareness that has increased in her through this experience is now affecting every aspect of her leadership and personal behaviour. Mindfulness is like turning on the light and exposing all our self-sabotaging beliefs that have been hidden for so long. It can be tough in the short term, but over the long term it always delivers greater integrity, peace and leadership effectiveness.

Changing deeply ingrained habits takes time

When psychologist Jeremy Dean started researching how long it takes for us to form or change a habit, he encountered the same magic number over and over: 21 days. Yet there was no concrete data to back up this widely held belief. So he explored the science and empirical data, which he published in his book *Making Habits, Breaking Habits: Why We Do Things, Why We Don't, and How to Make Any Change Stick.*

In one study carried out at University College London, 96 participants were asked to choose an everyday behaviour they wanted to turn into a habit, such as 'eating a piece of fruit with lunch' and 'running for 15 minutes after dinner'. For 84 days each subject logged into a website and reported whether or not they'd carried out the behaviour, as well as how automatic the behaviour had felt. It turns out that generally it takes much longer than 21 days to form a habit. Dean writes, '[O]n average, across the participants who provided enough data, it took sixty-six days until a habit was formed. As you might imagine, there was considerable variation in how long habits took to form depending on what people tried to do. People who resolved to drink a glass of water after breakfast were up to maximum automaticity after about twenty days, while those trying to eat a piece of fruit with lunch took at least twice as long to turn it into a habit. The exercise habit proved most tricky, with "fifty sit-ups after morning coffee" still not a habit after eighty-four days for one participant. "Walking for ten minutes after breakfast", though, was turned into a habit after fifty days for another participant.'

The results also showed that the early repetitions of an activity are most beneficial for establishing a habit and that gains gradually dwindle over time. As Dean explains, 'It's like trying to run up a hill that starts out steep and gradually levels off. At the start you're making great progress upwards, but the closer you get to the peak, the smaller the gains in altitude with each step.'

This is why, as I wrote in the introduction, our mindfulness practice must be sustained over time. We can't be present occasionally and expect to experience significant and long-lasting change. The formal practice of meditation is profoundly useful in this regard, as it allows us to be present continuously for long periods of time. And as we experience that, we're able to integrate it into our daily lives.

You are worth it

We've talked a lot about the toughness of change and the responsibility of leadership. You could be forgiven for feeling a little daunted by it all, but as I conclude this book I want to encourage you to persevere with a mindfulness practice.

First of all, it's important because you are worth it and you can make a difference. The practice itself is an affirmation of your value to yourself, a clear message that you matter, that your state of mind matters, that an open heart matters and that you can make a more positive difference in this world when you are mindful and grounded.

Secondly, it is an affirmation of care toward others. It is an acceptance that when you are in a clear and open-hearted state you impact others positively, therefore by taking care of your mind and heart, you are taking care of those you lead.

Thirdly, the practice makes such an amazing difference to your brain and your wellbeing. As the research shows, it can literally rewire your brain to enable you to think in more healthy and productive terms. It can make you smarter and more creative. It reduces your stress hormones, boosts your immune system, and improves your overall physical and mental health. As time passes we are finding more and more benefits of mindfulness.

Lastly, when we practise we become more available to the mystery, magic and majesty of life. A consistent reward of mindfulness is an inner sense of wellbeing that literally bursts out of us at times. We become a light in the world and for the world. The kind of light that all the darkness in the world cannot snuff out. This is the essence of great leadership and the kind of leadership that makes us all want to wake up to our best selves, to live and lead knowing each moment is precious, that it matters and our lives matter. I wish you the deepest happiness, knowing your happiness is not only precious to you but a gift to those whose lives you touch.

Acknowledgements

This book would never have happened were it not for the extraordinary mindfulness and inner-work teachers who have graced my life. You have challenged me to look deeper, supported me to be kinder and cared for me in my more fragile moments. You are my heroes, and the reason I fell in love with this work.

To you, Radha Nicholson, Subhana Barzaghi, Steven Smith, Russ Hudson, Don Riso, Anne Laney, Chris McClean, Shane Mulhall, Brian McGeough, Patrick Kearney, Margaret Coldwells, Barry Keesan, Marshall Rosenberg, Jim Kouzes and Barry Posner, and to my greatest teacher, my beloved wife Natasha Pilgrim, a deep bow of gratitude. I have been inspired by many others over the years, but you are the teachers I have personally worked with who have truly changed the trajectory of my life. Thank you.

Next I must thank the people I interviewed, who contributed to my understanding of how mindfulness really is the 'x-factor' in leadership. Many are mentioned by name in the text; others are not. I wholeheartedly thank each and every one of these individuals for sharing their experiences and insights.

I want to make special mention of a few people who supported the writing project itself:

- Jack Kornfield, for helping me find a kinder, cleaner writing style, especially in the opening chapters

- Subhana Barzaghi, for her technical mindfulness editing, proofreading, friendship and encouragement during this project

- Patrick Kearney, for his technical mindfulness editing, proofreading and wonderful interview contributions

- Steven Smith, for his proofreading of the book for mindfulness accuracy, and for teaching me about metta through his living example

- Jon Treanor and Laura Payne in the UK, for generously giving me access to some of their wonderful coaching clients, and for their amazing work in the field of mindful leadership

- Charlotte Thaarup-Owen, for giving me access to some of her wonderful clients, and for her amazing work in the field of mindfulnes

- Jay Coen Gilbert, who went above and beyond to support this project and who is an inspiration for a more conscious business world

- Barry Keesan, for his contributions to the book and introductions to other mindful leaders who have helped make the book so much better

- Spencer Sherman and Sue Kochan, for their contributions to the book and for introducing me to some special B Corp leaders

- Stephen Palmer, who brought order to the mountain of teaching transcriptions, notes and writing with which I began and then helped me structure and write a beautiful book. I count you as a dear friend.

- Justin Davis, for your brilliant research on the brain and mindfulness in general
- Edith Robb, for your comprehensive research on leadership and mindfulness
- Jim Kouzes and Barry Posner, for your boundless encouragement and support during the writing and for being so unbelievably generous with your time and your research. You guys really Model the Way.
- the wonderful, ordinary, extraordinary leaders who gave up their time to contribute to this book. You are all truly inspirational.
- those who took the time to write endorsements for the book, helping convince my readers it's worth reading.

I also want to thank Kristen Hammond, Senior Commissioning Editor with Wiley (Melbourne), for her kindness, unfailing support, flexibility and patience in guiding this manuscript from the editorial process through to production.

Thank you also to Ingrid Bond, Publishing Coordinator, and Chris Shorten, Project Editor, at Wiley Melbourne, for their superb support and craftsmanship throughout the editorial and publishing cycle.

Another deep bow of gratitude to Jem Bates, my editor, who did a fantastic job of culling excess content and making the book more readable in record time.

Notes

Introduction

1. Blodget, H. (2014, September 22). LinkedIn's CEO Jeff Weiner reveals the importance of body language, mistakes made out of fear, and one time he really doubted himself. *Business Insider.* Retrieved from www.businessinsider.com/linkedin-ceo-jeff-weiner-on-leadership-2014-9

2. Kouzes, J., & Posner, B. (2014). *Extraordinary Leadership in Australia & New Zealand: The Five Practices That Create Great Workplaces.*

3. Wenk-Sormaz, H. (2005). Meditation can reduce habitual responding. *Alternative Therapy Health Medicine, 11*(2), 42–58. Retrieved from www.ncbi.nlm.nih.gov/pubmed/15819448

4. Greenberg, J., Reiner, K., & Meiran, N. (2012). 'Mind the Trap': Mindfulness practice reduces cognitive rigidity. *PLOS ONE 7*(5), e36206. doi:10.1371/journal.pone.0036206

5. Dane, E., & Brummel, B. J. (2014). Examining workplace mindfulness and its relations to job performance and turnover intention. *Human Relations, 67*(1), 105–28. doi: 10.1177/0018726713487753

Chapter 1

1. Killingsworth, M. A., & Gilbert, D. T. (2010, November 12). A wandering mind is an unhappy mind. *Science, 330*(6006), 932. doi: 10.1126/science.1192439

2. Psychology Today,. (2016). The Embodied Mind. Retrieved 18 February 2016, from http://www.psychologytoday.com/blog/the-embodied-mind

3. While these four foundations are similar to the classic four foundations of mindfulness, I have not attempted to accurately represent the classic interpretation. I describe them this way to make them easily accessible for my clients and readers.

4. Notes from *Mindfulness Research Monthly, 1*(5), June 2010. Cover story by David S. Black, MPH, 'Hot topics: A 40-year publishing history of mindfulness'.

5. Notes from Kate Pickert, 'Mindfulness goes mainstream', *Time*, 3 February 2014.

6. Kasala, E. R., Bodduluru, L. N., Maneti, Y., & Thipparaboina, R. (2014). Effect of meditation on neurophysiological changes in stress mediated depression. *Complementary Therapies in Clinical Practice, 20*(1), 74–80. Jung, Y. H., Kang, D. H., Jang, J. H., Park, H. Y., Byun, M. S., Kwon, S. J., et al. (2010). The effects of mind–body training on stress reduction, positive affect, and plasma catecholamines. *Neuroscience Letters, 479*(2), 138–42.

7. Newberg, A. B., & Iversen, J. (2003). The neural basis of the complex mental task of meditation: Neurotransmitter and neurochemical considerations. *Medical Hypotheses, 61*(2), 282–91. Kasala, E. R., Bodduluru, L. N., Maneti, Y., & Thipparaboina, R. (2014). Effect of meditation on neurophysiological changes in stress mediated depression. *Complementary Therapies in Clinical Practice, 20*(1), 74–80.

8. Davidson, R. J., Kabat-Zinn, J., Schumacher, J., Rosenkranz, M., Muller, D., Santorelli, S. F., et al. (2003). Alterations in brain and immune function produced by mindfulness

meditation. *Psychosomatic Medicine, 65*(4), 564–70. Kasala, Bodduluru, Maneti & Thipparaboina, op. cit.

9. Tang, Y. Y., Hölzel, B. K., & Posner, M. I. (2015). The neuroscience of mindfulness meditation. *Nature Reviews Neuroscience, 16*(4), 213–25. Fox, K. C., Nijeboer, S., Dixon, M. L., Floman, J. L., Ellamil, M., Rumak, S. P., et al. (2014). Is meditation associated with altered brain structure? A systematic review and meta-analysis of morphometric neuroimaging in meditation practitioners. *Neuroscience & Biobehavioral Reviews, 43*, 48–73.

10. Lazar, S. W., Kerr, C. E., Wasserman, R. H., Gray, J. R., Greve, D. N., Treadway, M. T., et al. (2005). Meditation experience is associated with increased cortical thickness. *Neuroreport, 16*(17), 1893.

11. Tang, Y. Y., Lu, Q., Geng, X., Stein, E. A., Yang, Y., & Posner, M. I. (2010). Short-term meditation induces white matter changes in the anterior cingulate. *Proceedings of the National Academy of Sciences, 107*(35), 15649–52.

12. Tang, Y. Y., Hölzel, B. K., & Posner, M. I. (2015). The neuroscience of mindfulness meditation. *Nature Reviews Neuroscience, 16*(4), 213–25.

13. Tang, Y. Y., Rothbart, M. K., & Posner, M. I. (2012). Neural correlates of establishing, maintaining, and switching brain states. *Trends in Cognitive Sciences, 16*(6), 330–7.

14. Tang, Y. Y., Ma, Y., Wang, J., Fan, Y., Feng, S., Lu, Q., et al. (2007). Short-term meditation training improves attention and self-regulation. *Proceedings of the National Academy of Sciences, 104*(43), 17152–6. Tang, Hölzel & Posner, op. cit.

15. Sedlmeier, P., Eberth, J., Schwarz, M., Zimmermann, D., et al. (2012). The psychological effects of meditation: A meta-analysis. *Psychological Bulletin, 138*(8), 1139–71.

16. Wolever, R., Bobinet, K., McCabe, K., MacKenzie, L., Fekete, E., Kusnick, C., & Baime, M. (2012). Effective and

viable mind–body stress reduction in the workplace: Two RCTs. *Complementary and Alternative Medicine, 12*, 87.

17. Zeidan, F., Johnson, S. K., Diamond, B. J., David, Z., & Goolkasian, P. (2010). Mindfulness meditation improves cognition: Evidence of brief mental training. *Consciousness and Cognition, 19*(2), 597–605.

18. Moore, A., & Malinowski, P. Meditation, mindfulness, and cognitive flexibility. *Consciousness and Cognition. 18*, 176–86.

19. Hassed, C. The health benefits of meditation and being mindful. Monash University. Retrieved from www.yvg.vic.edu.au/file.php?fileID=5502

20. Greenberg, Reiner & Meiran (2012), op. cit.

21. Dekeyser, M., Raes, F., Leijssen, M., Leysen, S., & Dewulf, D. (2008). Mindfulness skills and interpersonal behavior. *Journal of Personality and Individual Differences, 44*(5), 1235–45.

22. Condon, P., Desbordes, G., Miller, W., & DeSteno, D. (2013). Meditation increases compassionate responses to suffering, *Journal of Psychological Science.* doi: 10.1177/0956797613485603

23. Davis, D. M., & Hayes, J. A. (2012, July/August). What are the benefits of mindfulness? *American Psychological Association, 43*(7).

24. Grossman, P., Niemann, L., Schmidt, S., & Walach, H. Mindfulness-based stress reduction and health benefits. Retrieved from www.ncbi.nlm.nih.gov/pubmed/15256293

Chapter 2

1. Achor, S. (2016). Transcript of "The happy secret to better work". Ted.com. Retrieved 18 February 2016, from http://www.ted.com/talks/shawn_achor_the_happy_secret_to_better_work/transcript?language=en

2. Centre for Clinical Interventions. (2016). Centre for Clinical Interventions (CCI) - Psychotherapy, Research, Training.

Retrieved 18 February 2016, from http://www.cci.health.
wa.gov.au/resources/infopax.cfm?Info_ID=54

3. Breines, J., & Chen, S. (2012). Self-Compassion Increases
   Self-Improvement Motivation. Personality And Social
   Psychology Bulletin, *38*(9), 1133–1143. http://dx.doi.
   org/10.1177/0146167212445599

Chapter 3

1. Prottas, D. J. (2013). Relationships among employee perception
   of their manager's behavioral integrity, moral distress, and
   employee attitudes and well-being, *Journal of Business Ethics*,
   113(1), 51–60.

2. Dahl, J., Plumb-Vilardaga, J., Stewart, I., & Lundgren, T.
   (2009). *The art and science of valuing in psychotherapy*, Oakland,
   CA: New Harbinger p. 1.

3. ibid., p. 9.

4. Bluett, E. J., Homan, K. J., Morrison, K. L., Levin, M. E., &
   Twohig, M. P. (2014). Acceptance and commitment therapy for
   anxiety and OCD spectrum disorders: An empirical review,
   Journal of Anxiety Disorders, 28(6), 612–24.

5. Quinlan, D., Swain, N., & Vella-Brodrick, D. A. (2012).
   Character strengths interventions: Building on what we know
   for improved outcomes, *Journal of Happiness Studies, 13*(6),
   1145–63.

6. Heckman, J. J., & Kautz, T. (2013). Fostering and measuring
   skills: Interventions that improve character and cognition,
   National Bureau of Economic Research, no. w19656.

7. Park, N., Peterson, C., & Seligman, M. E. (2004). Strengths of
   character and well-being, *Journal of Social and Clinical Psychology*,
   23(5), 603–19.

8. Kouzes & Posner, op. cit.

The Mindful Leader

9. Edelman Trust Barometer — Global Results (2014). Retrieved from www.slideshare.net/EdelmanInsights/2014-edelman-trust-barometer

10. Kiisel, T. (2013, January 30). 82 percent of people don't trust the boss to tell the truth, *Forbes*. Retrieved from www.forbes.com/sites/tykiisel/2013/01/30/82-percent-of-people-dont-trust-the-boss-to-tell-the-truth

Chapter 4

1. Gallup,. (2016). Worldwide, 13% of Employees Are Engaged at Work. Retrieved from http://www.gallup.com/poll/165269/worldwide-employees-engagedwork.aspx

2. Khan, M., Serafeim, G., & Yoon, A. (2015). Corporate Sustainability: First Evidence on Materiality. SSRN Electronic Journal. http://dx.doi.org/10.2139/ssrn.2575912

3. Goldman Sachs (2007, June 22). GS SUSTAIN, 12. Retrieved from www.natcapsolutions.org/business-case/GoldmanSachsReport_v2007.pdf

4. International Finance Corporation. (2012). The business case for sustainability 4. Retrieved from www.ifc.org/wps/wcm/connect/9519a5004c1bc60eb534bd79803d5464/Business%2BCase%2Bfor%2BSustainability.pdf?MOD=AJPERES

5. LaPlante, A. (2014). MBA Graduates Want to Work for Caring and Ethical Employers. Insights By Stanford Business. Retrieved from http://www.gsb.stanford.edu/insights/mba-graduates-want-work-caring-ethical-employers

6. Global Sustainable Investment Alliance,. (2014). 2014 Global Sustainable Investment Review. Retrieved from http://www.gsi-alliance.org/wp-content/uploads/2015/02/GSIA_ Review_download.pdf

Chapter 5

1. Chew, K. (2011). Why We Need To Encourage Curiosity In Students. care2. Retrieved from http://www.care2.com/causes/why-we-need-to-encourage-curiosity-in-students.html

2. Hafenbrack, A., Kinias, Z., & Barsade, S. (2013). Debiasing the Mind Through Meditation: Mindfulness and the Sunk-Cost Bias. *Psychological Science*, *25*(2), 369-376. http://dx.doi.org/10.1177/0956797613503853

3. Karelaia, N. & Reb, J., Improving Decision Making Through Mindfulness (2014). Forthcoming in *Mindfulness in Organizations*, Reb, J., & Atkins, P. (Eds.), Cambridge University Press.; INSEAD Working Paper No. 2014/43/DSC. http://ssrn.com/abstract=2443808

4. Snowden, D. J., & Boone, M. E. (2007, November). A leader's framework for decision making, *Harvard Business Review*.

5. Stillman, J. (2009). Five Mental Habits of Innovative People. CBS MoneyWatch. Retrieved from http://www.cbsnews.com/news/five-mental-habits-of-innovative-people/

Chapter 6

1. Mascaro, J. S., Rilling, J. K., Negi, L. T., & Raison, C. (2012). Compassion meditation enhances empathic accuracy and related neural activity, *Social Cognitive and Affective Neuroscience*, nss095.

2. Deloitte Access Economics,. (2016). The Collaborative Economy – unlocking the power of the workplace crowd. Retrieved from http://www2.deloitte.com/au/en/pages/economics/articles/collaborative-economy-unlocking-power-of-workplace-crowd.html

3. Zenger, J., & Folkman, J. (2013, September 11). 'Nice or tough: Which approach engages employees most?. *Harvard Business Review*.

Chapter 7

1. Jazaieri, H., McGonigal, K., Jinpa, T., Doty, J., Gross, J., & Goldin, P. (2013). A randomized controlled trial of compassion cultivation training: Effects on mindfulness, affect, and emotion regulation. *Motivation And Emotion, 38*(1), 23-35. http://dx.doi.org/10.1007/s11031-013-9368-z

2. Fredrickson, B., Cohn, M., Coffey, K., Pek, J., & Finkel, S. (2008). Open hearts build lives: Positive emotions, induced through loving-kindness meditation, build consequential personal resources. *Journal Of Personality And Social Psychology, 95*(5), 1045–1062. http://dx.doi.org/10.1037/a0013262

3. Davidson, R. (2010). Cultivating compassion: Neuroscientific and behavioral approaches, *Center for Compassion and Altruism Research and Education.*

4. Compassion Meditation May Improve Physical And Emotional Responses To Psychological Stress. (2008). ScienceDaily. Retrieved from https://www.sciencedaily.com/releases/2008/10/081007172902.htm

5. Ali, R., & Ahmed, M. S. (2009). The impact of reward and recognition programs on employees' motivation and satisfaction: An empirical study, *International Review of Business Research Papers, 5*(4), 270–9.

Chapter 8

1. Petrochko, C. (2013). Heart Patients Slow to Make Healthy Choices. MedPage Today. Retrieved from http://www.medpagetoday.com/Cardiology/Prevention/38498

Index

Connect
with WILEY ▶▶▶

WILEY

Browse and purchase the full range of Wiley publications on our official website.

www.wiley.com

Check out the Wiley blog for news, articles and information from Wiley and our authors.

www.wileybizaus.com

Join the conversation on Twitter and keep up to date on the latest news and events in business.

@WileyBizAus

Sign up for Wiley newsletters to learn about our latest publications, upcoming events and conferences, and discounts available to our customers.

www.wiley.com/email

Wiley titles are also produced in e-book formats. Available from all good retailers.

WILEY

Learn more with practical advice from our experts

Extraordinary Leadership in Australia and NZ
James Kouzes and Barry Posner with Michael Bunting

The Leadership Challenge
James Kouzes and Barry Posner

The Student Leadership Challenge
James Kouzes and Barry Posner

How to Lead a Quest
Dr Jason Fox

Humanise
Anthony Howard

Future Brain
Dr Jenny Brockis

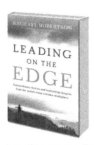

Leading on the Edge
Rachael Robertson

Doing Good by Doing Good
Peter Baines

Conscious Marketing
Carolyn Tate

Available in print and e-book formats

WILEY